The SMARTASS® Recruiter

Jackie Handy

Copyright

Acknowledgements

As you read on, you'll see where the inspiration for writing this book came from. Put simply, without the experiences I've encountered over the years both operationally and in my training consultancy work, this book would never have been written.

So to all I've have worked with, worked for and worked alongside in this wonderful industry of recruitment, I thank you.

I believe that every great thing and every hiccup on this journey of life brings us to precisely where we need to be at any given moment in time. I've had huge successes and monumental catastrophes in my working life over the years and I realise that to truly differentiate between the two we must experience both. That's precisely when we become rounded individuals who make different, more conscious decisions. And somewhere in the midst of the darkest moments, Purpose lights a pathway forward.

So to the Universe, thank you for the darkness as well as for the light.

JACKIE HANDY

Dedication

This book is for Shar.

My whole world

JACKIE HANDY

So you think you're a

recruitment consultant?

"I know that I am intelligent, because I know that I know nothing. "

Socrates

If you're reading this then thank you for choosing this book from the vast array of self-help and recruitment guru books. I'll pretty much guarantee you won't thank me as you start reading this book (and possibly throughout it!), but by the end of it, you'll get it – maybe. I intend to be candid and no-nonsense in my opinions, but through it all I'll be giving valuable advice for new or aspiring recruitment consultants as well as some powerful reminders to those of you with experience in the field.

So who am I?

I've worked in recruitment since the late 90's both as a Recruitment Consultant and Manager and in recent years as a self-employed consultant and trainer. During my lengthy recruitment career, I regularly topped the league tables in my company and more than once tripled my salary year on year, in bonus payments. It's taken time to get to the position I'm in now. Despite the fact that the role of a recruitment consultant appears relatively simple, it took me time to truly get to grips with the core principles of successful recruiting. Furthermore to implement them thoroughly and consistently, enabling me to have an easy to repeat recipe for success. A recipe I'm about to share with you in this book. Despite my success, I made many mistakes. In fact I made some monumental corkers. I now devote my life to 'giving back' in the hope that far less of you make the mistakes I did and achieve success a whole lot sooner.

Of course this isn't about me. What is important is the fact that the recruitment industry has huge opportunities to offer you and loads of money available for you to earn. So I ask you, "What's stopping you making some serious money?"

The industry is getting battered right now with criticisms of shoddy business practices. We're called out again and again on unethical behaviour from recruitment consultants who, frankly, don't give a fuck about candidates and clients and I say "enough is enough".

There are some great people out there in recruitment, all of whom want to earn a living in a professional and savvy way.

Plenty of people are quick to moan and whine without truly understanding what recruiters go through day-by-day, week on week, and month on month. As far as I'm concerned there are far too many people throwing stones from afar (or from behind a computer screen) and they should think about getting their own houses in order first.

However as I climb back down from my soap box I realise it has to be said; sometimes these vile recruiter-hating trolls have a point.

Every year I train 'you people' all over the world. Cultures may be vastly different, but the principles of successful contingency recruitment are fundamentally the same.

The main thing that I see over and over, is that you aren't actually doing a whole lot with what you are learning. I, and countless others like me, are giving you the tools but for some unexplained reason, those workbooks that you all know and love and promise to revisit, still end up in the bin. Or at best in your filing tray, gathering dust, covered up with endless CVs and 'stuff' that you'll never get round to doing anything properly with.

What is stopping you using these tools?

I don't believe people are inherently lazy. I think there are 2 reasons people don't 'do' what they should. Either they don't know what to do or they don't see any value and benefit in doing it. If you've been given the tools from any form of eLearning, classroom training, seminar or desk training from your line manager then I can only assume that, if you haven't put your learning in to practice, you thought it had no value.

So that tells me the training didn't engage you, the trainer was dull or you suffered from a total lack of interest. If you're reading this I'm going to go out on a limb and suggest it wasn't the latter. As a passionate training consultant, it hurts my heart to tell you that up to 70% of what we learn in the classroom we forget. Pretty sad statistic, huh? And why is that? For many of the reasons above, plus the most important factor. You don't even start putting it into practice. You are unsupported when you return from your training and so simply go back to 'business as usual' and as I often say, "if nothing changes, then nothing changes".

"Oh to have training" I hear some of you cry. Don't tell me, you have transferable skills, you fell into recruitment and you are expected to 'hit the ground running' simply by copying the behaviour of another average recruiter who "learned" his recruitment skills from the last poor sod.

I call this the "eat, sleep, LEAVE, repeat" method of screwing up the industry. Feel free to pass this book on to your boss after you've read it, they might learn something too. But in fairness to them they can't do it for you. Only you can put in the graft and focus on the correct activities to be truly successful. It's undoubtedly a huge plus if you have their support, but not a necessity.

All in all, the industry is in a challenging place. The global economy isn't particularly stable right now. Trump, Brexit, terrorism, the threat of nuclear war etc., alongside a shortage of skilled workers, which only makes matters worse.

These challenges may be out there but that doesn't mean we can't be successful recruiters. These are not excuses for poor results or unethical behaviour. After all, organisations are still recruiting staff. So instead you need to think about how to adapt your style to this new economic climate.

And if nothing changes, nothing changes, right?

Doing my bit to sort this mess out gave me the inspiration to write this book. I'm giving this stuff away in a last, desperate attempt to get you motivated, to change, ditch or refine what you do in order for you to be a successful recruiter. Call it a reference manual, your personal workbook, a story or a godsend. Call it what you like but read it, enjoy it and take time to reflect on what you want to achieve, s well as what you can do differently in your

work. But most important of all, bloody well use the tips!
Look out for the special

'Handy Hint' sections throughout this book.

They highlight some nuggets of pure recruitment gold.
There are also extra blank pages at the rear of the book for
your own notes.

This book is written for temporary, permanent, contract or
360 contingency recruiters or aspiring recruiters. Those
who really want to excel in the industry. I've warned you
that I'm going to be candid and no-nonsense (you may
already have realised this), so if you don't like it then feel
free to close the book and keep on keeping on 'oh Average
one', or better still, get the hell out of recruitment and find
another job that'll be gentler on you and simply pay you a
regular wage. If you choose the latter, I'd suggest you apply
to jobs directly rather than approach a recruitment agency
– most recruiters are crap.

What makes a recruitment consultant?

"May your choices
reflect your hopes,
not your fears."

Nelson Mandela

THE SMARTASS RECRUITER

If you are to believe everything you read in the press then it's 'arrogance, cockiness and an air of self-importance'. However, my own experience suggests that you're generally a great bunch of people who want to do well, but just don't always know how to. If you do know, then it's either that something is stopping you putting your knowledge into practice or you've cleverly concealed that you are exactly as the press describes...

Perhaps instead I should have entitled this chapter 'What makes a *great* recruitment consultant?' as that's what I'm actually trying to convey and am keen to explore in more depth.

In my humble opinion, academic qualifications, degrees and the like aren't a prerequisite for a great recruitment consultant.

I guess I would say that wouldn't I, given I don't have a degree!

I'm not suggesting it wouldn't be a 'nice to have' (especially if it aligns with the recruitment sector you choose); just that it's not essential. I've worked with many people over the years. Qualified accountants who recruit for accountants, qualified carpenters who supply to the construction industry, those with teaching qualifications who support the education sector. While these are undoubtedly useful extras to have, they won't automatically create success in a recruitment role.

What a great recruiter actually needs is a positive attitude and to really appreciate how they make a difference to the lives of others, through the service they provide. I call this: **Career Purpose.**

In case you feel I'm going all deep and fluffy on you, I'm not (well, not entirely). I mean simply, that a great recruitment consultant will be able to clearly articulate what gets them up in the morning, what inspires them to perform and what gets them back on the bike after been pushed off it time and time again.

And please don't give me that same old 1980's reply of "I'm in it for the money" because a) that's bullshit and b) that's bullshit.

Disclaimer – I know I wrote it twice. That tells you how much I think it's a bullshit answer.

If you're challenging my thinking, then you need this book more than I thought. Maybe your boss is looking for money-driven people (pass the book over please), but honestly, show me someone who wouldn't be. Show me one person in the world who isn't driven in some way, by money.

Go!

If you do find someone then the chances are they already have money and probably a lot of it. Therefore, they don't count because before they had it, it played its part in driving them too.

Career Purpose is beyond money; it's the answer to the questions, "what's it all about for me?", "why do I do, what I do?" and "how do I make a difference?". It's much more than money.

It's what money *allows us to do* that drives us, rather than the money itself. Money alone does *not* motivate us. Oh and that's a fact by the way. Google it.

Yes, a great recruiter needs:-

resilience | tenacity | commercial acumen | communication skills | empathy | selfishness – yes that even ranks in there.

Those are all important components to being successful in this field – and there are many more. But if you don't know *why* you do what you do and aspire to fulfilling your Career Purpose (at least in your current role), then it's a certainty that you'll only be, at best, an average recruiter.

Be honest with yourself. You're reading this and realising that you don't have a Career Purpose. And that's ok because, despite what you might think, I'm actually writing this book to help you. A Career Purpose isn't always immediately apparent, especially if it hasn't been given any real thought. Remember this is your Career Purpose, not your Life Purpose. I'm not interested in hearing how you want to be "the flame that ignites world peace" or anything as profound.

You are not Ghandi. (And if you are, recruitment probably

isn't your calling.)

Naturally if you *do* have a Life Purpose then great, but don't think having one is crucial to your success at work. It isn't. Instead I want you to think about what your purpose is as a recruitment consultant. How you want others to view you, a descriptor of the

Values that shape how you work and a summary for what you'd like others say about you when you're not in the room.

This is actually quite an interesting practical to do. Imagine how your colleague would answer if they were asked to describe you and how you do your job?

Defining a Career Purpose can take a while, so give yourself time to think about it. Continue reading this book and gather inspiration from my words combined with your thoughts as you read. The company you work for (or aspire to work for) might have some Values that give you some inspiration too. But don't just copy and paste them, that's lazy and precisely one of things people hate in a recruiter! Instead put your own spin on them as you consider what you want your Career Purpose to be. That's 'smart lazy' and that's a perfectly acceptable trait to have in recruitment.

Once you've given that some consideration, the next step is to think about your personal **Values**. These are the behaviours and traits that you believe define you and the way you work in the way you do.

Some of mine include:

Passion – I believe in doing what you do wholeheartedly or not at all.
Service – I believe that serving others deeply, sincerely and without judgement, plays a vital role in self-fulfilment.
Humour – I believe laughter and fun are fundamental to the journey of fulfilment

I have seven Values in total and I'd recommend a number somewhere between five and eight. Too few Values and you restrict yourself too much. Too many Values and it can be easy to lose track of the core of the exercise. Your Values should be from within and be part of you. If they're not then you're really only lying to yourself and making it pointless to do. For instance having a value of "integrity" may fit your Career Purpose seamlessly but have no real function if you lie and cheat your way through your career.

The next step is creating goals. Goals that align with your Career Purpose and Values and, possibly (added bonus) those of your employer.
If you're already a recruiter, chances are you've heard of the good old acronym SMART for goal setting?

THE SMARTASS RECRUITER

It stands for:

Specific

Measurable

Achievable or Attainable

Relevant or Realistic

Time bound

If you haven't heard of it or don't understand how it works, fear not, I'll cover it here for you. Even if you have heard of it, why not take some time to refresh your knowledge of it. Have you been working SMART up to now?

The SMART goals acronym has been around since the early 80's and there have been some adaptations added over the years. SMARTER, SMARTEST etc. All are similar in their principles, yet for me there are still some clear parts to goal-setting that are missing. I'll explain.
In order to firstly demonstrate the SMART goal-setting model, let me first make the distinction between a traditional non-SMART and SMART goal with this example:

Non-SMART: I want to get fit

I haven't defined what 'fit' is so can't measure anything, I don't know if it's achievable or relevant and I haven't set a timeframe for starting (or completing) the task.

Compare this to:

SMART: I want to be able to run a marathon in under 4.5 hours by July 2020

See the difference?

It is specific which means that, consequentially I can measure my progress towards achieving it. It is relevant to my 'getting fit' situation and it's humanly possible. Finally there are 2 timeframes attached to it – the time I take to run the marathon, and by when.

BUT, and here's the difference. It's not truly authentic for me if it doesn't Align with my Career Purpose, so this will hinder my engagement to this goal. If I don't connect my goals to my overall 'why' I'm left with a feeling of disconnection. As with all goals I need to be prepared to make the Sacrifices I need to make in order to achieve that; in the case of marathon running perhaps quitting smoking would be beneficial, being prepared to run in all weathers and potentially taking time away from my family in order to do so. If I'm not prepared to make some form of

Sacrifice I will absolutely not achieve this goal. We rarely achieve our goals single-handedly so undoubtedly without some form of Support I will also struggle to stay focused and achieve my goal. Incidentally the support we may need could come from a person or a resource.

I'm secretly pleased about this, as I hate running. With. A. Passion.

You on the other hand, might have a goal like this in mind (you crazy running freak you). If your Values and Career Purpose align to make this a real possibility for you, then you can correctly suggest it's authentic for you, but now give extra thought to the Sacrifice you'll need to make and how you'll need to be Supported in order to achieve it.

Given so many of us set SMART goals in business and these miss these vital elements of Alignment, Sacrifice and Support, I think there's more to be added, so I'm introducing a new model.

It is:

Specific

Measurable

Achievable

Relevant

Time bound

Alignment

Sacrifice

Supported

Or **SMARTASS** for short

You love it right?

All this talk of marathon running is exhausting, so let's consider a work example of a SMARTASS goal:

Imagine my Career Purpose is: To be a distinctive, consistently high performing recruitment professional My SMARTASS goal might read like this: By the end of (insert month/year here) to have increased my candidate pipeline by (insert number of candidates) through dedicating my next four Sunday afternoons to social media networking and out-of-hours candidate registrations.

Notice the traditional SMART element in the example first, and how it allows me to cover my ASS (so to speak).

This goal would be Aligned with my Career Purpose. In other words, having this goal supports my wider intention so it's authentic. It also encourages me to consider the Sacrifice (in this case four Sunday afternoons) I'm prepared to make in order to achieve it. In addition, I would consider at the time of setting the goal, the Support I would need to achieve it (i.e. the 'okay' from the other half, system access from my employer and a suitable place to meet candidates).

You see how it sometimes pays to be a SMARTASS? (Or at least it does when it comes to goal setting).

Another final thing to consider about goals and it's a pretty important consideration.

There is much evidence to suggest that goals don't work. Yes you read that right – goals don't work.

Now you think *I'm* the SMARTASS.

In case you're wondering why the hell I've let you read this section before letting you know, then I'll elaborate.

Firstly, have you ever set a goal and not achieved it? Had a New Year resolution that you gave up on before February? Yes? Then there's the proof, right there.

Secondly, goals are often set so far in the future that they seem unattainable. We often find ourselves attaching labels such as 'happiness' and 'success' to the achievement of a goal. Ever find yourself saying, "When I reach that goal, I'll be happy"? "When I do this I'll be successful"? Now, just take a moment to think about that…

If you're attaching your 'happy' or your 'successful' to something way over there in goal-land, then surely that suggests you can't be happy or feel successful right now? And if you aren't happy or feeling successful now you can be sure you won't be in the right headspace to create any decent goals in the first place, let alone hope to achieve anything!

There's a fabulous book written by the wonderful Eckhart Tolle entitled 'The Power of Now' that illustrates this beautifully. It's a rather deep read but one that demonstrates how to attach emotions to the only true place you can – in the present. So you need to somehow stretch yourself but in a way that allows you to experience positive emotions right now.

So without discrediting everything I've just written about goals and being a SMARTASS etc. I'll give you my take on it. I agree with the statement and all the Harvard-based research around the fact that goals don't work. In my opinion, there's one word missing. Alone.

"Goals **alone** don't work"

You need to be equally able to attach a level of happiness or success to the here and now right? That's why in order to really smash your goals out of the park (which will undoubtedly be aided by adding your ASS to your SMART), alongside a great SMARTASS goal you should also make a daily **Step Plan**. I don't mean a call list/KPI-type plan. I mean a commitment to do something, *anything*, each day that will take you towards your goal.

Consider it being simply the very next thing that you need to do, to start to make your goal a reality.
Why? Because nothing happens without action.

A Step Plan will help you start taking the relevant actions to lead you closer to your goals. Then you can actually start to enjoy the goal-setting journey, rather than setting goals you think you should set simply because that's what you're supposed to do. You can feel accomplished after each small step you take, knowing you are making headway towards your goal. You stop just doing and start doing with Purpose. Having a Step Plan also means that, if things change to potentially knock you off course or you realise that something needs refining, you are on top of it immediately rather than finding out a month or two down the line that you're way off track.

So let's go back to the original SMARTASS goal that we set in our example; what would some of the things be that you could commit to each day in order to achieve this? What actions could form your Step Plan?

Join some relevant LinkedIn groups perhaps? Post an article or a blog online to get yourself noticed? Source a local venue to meet your candidates? Sort your remote system access out in advance with your IT department? Book a restaurant to take your other half to Sunday dinner as payback for their support during one of the days? And so on.

Without getting deep again, achieving goals is a journey and every journey is achieved through steps taken – the right steps. That's how a Step Plan works - you basically start walking!

In the hope that, at least something has hit home here, I've intentionally left some space in case you want to note:

Your Career Purpose (when you have it defined):

_____

_____

_____

_____

_____

Your Values:

_____

_____

_____

_____

_____

A SMARTASS goal:

_____

_____

_____

_____

_____

Your Step Plan:

_____

_____

_____

_____

_____

CVSS, unintentional recruitment-based coincidence there methinks!

I'd recommend you start this before we move on . There's a whole lot more coming in the next chapters and even though CVSS will be forever imprinted on your brain, trust me, you'll forget lots of this by the time you're half way in.

Oh and by the way, my

Handy Hint

"Get all this in order
and just watch the money
follow..."

Industry Sector, Temp or Perm?

"We have true control
over only two moments
in our lives..

Here and Now"

Unknown

I'm often asked by recruitment consultants "which sector is best?" and "where can I be most successful – temp or perm?"

Honestly, there's no right or wrong answer here. No better or worse response I can give. Each and every sector and desk has its advantages and disadvantages and like everything in recruitment, your desk will ultimately be a reflection of your efforts.

It *is* however; fair to say that some sectors will have many more legalities to consider. Education, healthcare and so on. You should also perhaps consider whether you'd prefer a blue or white-collar industry.

Fundamentally the contrasts are typically: high volume, low margin vs. low volume, high margin. I don't feel either is better than the other. I guess the question is, "do you want to deal with lots of people, lots of paperwork & general administration but work quickly and have lots of low value bookings?" or "do you want to have to spend lots of time sourcing candidates and approaching passive candidates to encourage them to work with you on a smaller number of roles, but roles that will make you a whole load of commission?"

Once you answer those questions you'll have part of your answer. Naturally if you have a degree (as mentioned earlier) or some professional experience, it would be useful to consider recruiting in that  sector. You'll already have valuable insight into the jargon and will shortcut your own desk set up somewhat. It'll possibly also align more authentically with your Career Purpose and your SMARTASS goals will prove much easier to draft.

If like me, you fell into recruitment from some random, totally unconnected job then consider instead your personal qualities and working style. As I mentioned earlier there is some research to suggest that selfishness is a great trait to have in permanent recruitment (but that doesn't mean you have to be an asshole). My thoughts are that recruitment is what recruitment is.

All recruitment consultants should behave with a sense of care and concern to both client & candidate and all should be happy to get on the phone; I mean really get on the phone.

As you read on you'll see my take on 'cold-calling', which is that, there should actually be very little. But that doesn't

negate the need to actually dial out, a lot, every day. You have to kiss a lot of frogs in this game to find your prince(ss) and if you're in any doubt about how hard it can be, I'm telling you now, it can be really hard. Even more so if you're not focused on your outcomes. And that's why you need to keep your Career Purpose, Values and your SMARTASS goals at the forefront of everything you do.

Recruitment Consultants also need an element of organisation and time management. Given time management is another topic I'm frequently asked about, it seems most of us (including me) are pretty crap at it. To help I've written a chapter all about it which we'll get to later. I tell my training groups there is no magic wand. Let's face it, everyone has the same amount of hours in the day, so why is it that some people achieve amazing results while the rest of us run around like headless chickens and achieve less?

One of the key reasons has to be Career Purpose my friends, plain and simple. Most of us do what we do each day because we're told to and we reluctantly accept it as part of our job (i.e. the dreaded KPI), yet somehow doing that removes our brain and prevents us thinking logically and rationally about whether that is actually achieving what we need it to achieve. If you don't even have a Career Purpose, personal Values or a SMARTASS goal then how can you even start to answer that question? Impossible isn't it. That's why so many recruitment consultants end up being puppets with the KPI-masters controlling the strings.

Handy Hint

One thing, arguably the most important thing you need to be asking yourself about everything you do is this,

"Does doing this take me closer to my desired outcome?"

It's a simple yes/no answer. If yes, then do it. If no, then do something else that does.

I'm realistic enough to know that not every single task that must be done will lead you *directly* towards your outcomes. I mean exactly how does dealing with processing a holiday pay telephone request for Janice Smith help get you closer to your Career Purpose of 'To be a distinctive, consistently high performing professional' as per our earlier example? So look beneath the surface of the task. Janice isn't intentionally crushing your daily call time with an annoying interruptions is she? She doesn't know that despite it being Thursday at 3pm, you've still only hit 10% of your entire weeks KPIs does she? So give her a break and remember what's really important to you...

Firstly, if you want to be distinctive then be remembered for giving great service. Janice is a current worker after all and you have a duty of care to look out for her. Secondly, if you don't sort it, Janice will likely tell you to 'shove your role where the sun don't shine', leave you and your role and tell everyone she possibly can about how crap you are. You lose on billings and on reputation. Is that really how a 'consistently high performing professional' behaves? Doubtful. But then if you hadn't decided on your Career Purpose be honest, you'd probably have avoided the call, asked someone else to deal with it or simply made a note and forgotten about it.

Cue another industry battering LinkedIn thread.
Now you may know that if you're successful in placing temporary workers you'll eventually be blessed with 'rolling revenue'* month on month. In other words you won't start each month on £0 (null points) and that will help get you a head start to your commission threshold. Sounds good doesn't it?

But make no mistake; you'll earn every penny with calls (from Janice & co), reference checks and compliance, no-shows and the like. Nobody gets money for nothing in this game.

---

* *If you're very new to recruitment or about to embark on a career in recruitment, the term 'rolling revenue' basically means that, when you place temporary workers who will work for a number of weeks, they will submit timesheets for payment through you and your company. Once they have been paid for their hours worked and your costs are deducted, the profit will roll week on week for you to include with your revenue figures and for you to calculate your commission.*

Unless you are the 'pipeline king/queen', you'll always be on a standing start on a perm desk, but you'll need fewer high-value placements to make some serious  commission. The placement journey can take longer, you'll have notice periods and start date changes to manage, so will need to have some great control mechanisms in place to ensure those offers turn into starts. It's a huge kick in the teeth when, after all that effort, interview co-ordination and feedback, it all comes to nothing – think carefully.

In summary, do your homework on industry sector and temp/perm split. I've met many recruitment consultants over the years who really can't cut the sector they're in, yet they do have the right skills for recruitment. It's got to be a nature/nurture argument really. Either you just don't have the attributes required to succeed in a particular field or that potential hasn't had the opportunity to come through yet.

Ask for support, take responsibility for your knowledge, demand the skills training you need to succeed and don't be too proud to change sectors if you need to. Better that than you wing it and blag it all the way to your P45.

Let's wrap this bit up in some more reflection. Use the space on the following pages to answer honestly about yourself:

What are my personal qualities? (Nature)

Where are my gaps that need bridging? (Nurture)

What do I enjoy spending my time doing? (Step Plan)

What's important to me? (Career Purpose)

Made your decision? Good – let's move on

The recruiter's marketplace

"Caring is a powerful business advantage."

Scott Johnson

Regardless of sector and whether you specialise on temp or perm roles (or both), you simply have to understand your

market. Clients and candidates are frankly pissed off with half-assed recruitment consultants talking rubbish to them on the phone because they haven't done their research.

You might think that you sound great, can make engaging small talk and are totally likeable and you've spent your business life being told, "People buy from people".

Well here's the truth... they don't.

This statement is in fact incomplete, not bullshit, just incomplete. People actually buy from people they TRUST and that only happens if you can demonstrate you are trustworthy. In business this doesn't mean 'smile when you dial' and similar old hat drivel. Instead it means you talk *their* language and you give them what they need. Are you getting me? The only way you can do that is to truly understand your market.

The market has many facets –

- clients
- candidates
- competitors
- colleagues.

There's another important 'c' word in recruitment (not what you're thinking!), but we'll come to that later. Let's start by looking at the basics of what you should know about each of these:

Clients – Who are they, where are they, what do they do, what technology do they use, what attributes do they look for in their employees, what are their company Values, how do they recruit, why do they recruit that way, what positions do they struggle to recruit for?

At very least you need to have these basic questions answered and you should use everything in your power to get them. With today's technology it really isn't difficult. Their own website, candidates you have registered who work/have worked for them, Glassdoor, LinkedIn, Facebook, Twitter etc. are simple, yet effective places to start. When you hit stuff you don't understand, Google it, ask a colleague, ask a candidate, but find out! Asking a client for basic market info about your 'specialist' sector is the quickest route to looking a complete donut and you'll likely be remembered for all the wrong reasons.

Cue another industry bashing LinkedIn thread.

Candidates – What does a great candidate in your sector look like? Skill sets, qualifications, work history, technologies used, achievements and so on. What represents a great 'opportunity' for candidates in your sector – Long-term work? Remuneration? Progression? Particular 'sexy' projects? What really drives them? I.e. their Values and motivational drivers. What is their Career Purpose?

Again, at very least you should be able to answer these questions. Otherwise you'll only ever be fighting your competitor on price and that's really poor recruiting. Besides, once you know this info, you'll start to see which candidates are more available than others and start to make plans to find those more elusive candidates too! Similarly, use your existing candidate database, your colleagues and the world-wide-web to find this stuff out. Especially if you're in a sector whereby particular experience or qualifications are a pre-requisite. You need to really know the things that will make a good role a great role for candidates – that's how you'll make your marketing stand out to them

Competitors – time and time again I scrutinise consultants about their competition and time and time again they fail dismally in their knowledge of them. Answer me this; how the hell can you know the solution you are offering is good if you don't know what your competition is doing?

According to Companies House, nearly 3,000 recruitment agencies launched in the first half of 2016. Yes you heard that right – the first *half* of 2016. If just 1% of them covered your sector that's another 30 potential competitors you have just in a 6-month period.

Naturally you should be telling me you already knew that, but you didn't did you?

How often do you check out your competitors' websites? Their top consultant's? Their current business services and offering's? Their price points? Their top client's? Why people buy from them? Their weaker areas? How often do you and your colleagues discuss this information as a team to build up a picture of your competition?

Handy Hint

The old saying is still relevant – Keep your friends close and your enemies closer.

For certain if you don't, it'll bite you on the bum in the future. Research them, mystery shop them if you have to because this information could be crucial to your success. Don't underestimate the importance of this task. Oh and chances are, you've been mystery shopped by them in the past too – would you and your business have had them worried?

Colleagues – Maybe you wouldn't have naturally included 'colleagues' as one of the market components, but knowing who's who in your network can make your life a whole lot easier in recruitment.

Who does what in your team?

Who's who in your division?

Who are the key contacts in your company?

Who are the people I really need to be known to? I'm not referring to the CEO (although that's useful). I mean who's in temp payroll?

Who controls the company's marketing budget?

Who pays you? (Very important).

Who has industry/client/candidate/competitor knowledge that you don't have? And what about the other divisions/sub-sections of your business that you could pass opportunities to?

Yes it's true that you may actually pass a lead and (huge gasp) not get any commission for it – I know, what an injustice! It still astounds me how so many recruiters still have this small-minded approach of actually preferring their own company to miss out, simply because passing leads and referrals won't directly affect their own back pocket. Seriously, what are you thinking??? In today's economy, more so now than ever before, it is vital you start becoming more globalised in your thinking. You remember how many competitors are opening up don't you? 3000 in the first 6 months of 2016 alone. Any one of them happy to take that lead you didn't see fit to pass to a colleague within your own company.

If your competitors are getting opportunities that your business is missing out on, that will affect your own businesses profitability. That will absolutely influence your pay rise, your commission structure, your promotional prospects and even your job security. C'mon guys grow a pair please and get commercial about this. I said earlier that selfish isn't meant to mean being an asshole and this is an example of what I mean by that. Be selfish on behalf of your business yes, but personal short-sightedness when it comes to ignoring leads? That's being an asshole!

Ok, so now we've covered the basics lets cover a few more.

The Market: Mapping

Mapping out your market is a term we use often in recruitment. Usually you'll be given an area, most of the time within either a niche industry sector or geographical boundary, or both.

Typically, what follows is the intention to analyse your existing database of clients in that remit and the candidates you have registered. You intend to categorise them in order of value and take a well thought through, targeted approach to maximise opportunities, skyrocketing you to the top of the company league table.

And then shit happens...

If you're new, you'll be busy being 'inducted' via show rounds, colleague shadowing, training courses (if you're one of the lucky ones) and navigating a new CRM database system. The focus will undoubtedly be getting you on the phone as quickly as possible. Let's face it, you've undergone a 3 month long, 5 phase interview, assessment day, psychometric profile, meet the team, wipe your ass, kiss my ass recruitment process. Now your company wants its pound of flesh.

If you're not new then frankly, you're probably already in a mess with your market mapping.

Handy Hint

Mapping your market well
at the outset will take
some investment of your
time, but will pay
dividends in the long
run.

The old phrase 'fail to plan, plan to fail' springs to mind here.

Tell me how many calls do you find yourself making to companies who have 3 staff members and tend to use the owners wife's best friends aunt, Marjorie, to assist them if they need help? I've done it and more than once too, probably tens of times over the years. Much as I've attempted to salvage my ineptitude by questioning around what happens if Marjorie is ill, that 'if one person leaves that's a third of their workforce they are down' blah blah, you know as well as I do that that is lame.

So you either need to hope your company gives you some time out of your first few weeks to segment and map out your client and candidate databases (good luck with that), or like the rest of us you get things in order over your lunch break, after hours etc. There's a rather cheesy phrase we use in recruitment, "treat your desk like your own business" and this 'in your own time' mapping is one example of what is meant by it.

If I'd left my day job to launch my business with no leads, network or strategy to get some, I'd have fallen flat on my face before I started. Yet sadly I see so many recruiters falling flat for lots of different reasons. But lack of planning is definitely near the top of that list.

There are a number of ways to map your market and for the purpose of this book; I'm going to keep it simple for you. Split it into 3 categories – Past, Present, Future. Let me expand on this.

Past – these are clients/candidates who you or your company has worked with in the past but are no longer dealing with.

There will likely be one of three reasons they are past relationships;

1. One off need or isolated placement (the Marjorie clients and candidates),
2. Your competitors gave them more,
3. You or your company pissed them off

With your 'Marjorie' clients consider whether there will be future growth plans and let that determine the level of contact you have with them.

With 'Marjorie' candidates, how long term is/was that role? When are they likely to move again? Could they be a hiring manager? Could they refer you to a hiring manager? The answers you receive here will, once again, determine the type and frequency of contact you should have with them.

Be sure you stay in touch appropriately and don't allow them to fall into reasons 2 or 3

If they already fall into reason 2, then you need to find out what specifically the 'more' was that they received from the competitor. Perhaps something as simple as more contact received or as complex as a more inclusive RPO (Recruitment Process Outsourcing – Google it!) solution was offered. I importantly refer back to the earlier comments of knowing your competitor offering inside out! At very least you'll need to be able to match what they now receive to woo them back to you. Maybe the hiring manager has changed? Worth pointing out that reasons 2 and 3 are often connected, and if they are then your journey to reconvert them will be all the more difficult. The same applies to your candidates – what are other agencies offering them that you're not? That's what you need to tap into and build upon if you're going to stand any chance of converting them.

Reason 3's are difficult, especially if it was someone else in your company and they have now left. Easy to blame them though, right? Wrong! You (or the other person) represented your brand – criticise them, you criticise your brand. I'd advise an honest apology and a sincere keenness to prove yourself and your company again. Of course, I'm assuming you want that business or that candidate back? Whether you do or not is for you to decide. And if you do, expect to work for it! Recruiters are so quick to find excuses for what went wrong. Put yourself in the clients/candidates shoes – how refreshing would it be for someone to just accept they made a mistake? After all, don't we all make mistakes? The trick is to learn from them and not repeat the cock up in the future. Communicate appropriately, fulfil your promises and accept bridges take time to build. I'll talk more on this when we look at Blockers further in.

Present – These are your current clients or your active candidates. Do NOT be complacent. Care for them, go out of your way for them and always look for ways to build upon the relationship. With your clients consider who are the other hiring managers you could be introduced to. Who could your colleagues support from other divisions? I'm 100% certain that your competitors are schmoozing these guys ready to sweep them from underneath you. Keep tight with your current clients. What else (other than recruitment) is happening with your clients? Are they launching a new product, attending events etc.? Take an interest and be sure to give value in everything you do. You don't always have to physically ask for business, instead behave like the trusted partner your clients want from a recruiter. Likewise, for your candidates – they have a life outside of their work – take an interest in it. Keep tight with them, and communicate frequently. By phone, by dropping in to see them at work, by meeting for coffee. Much as you may think yourself indispensable, you're not. But you should act in such a way that you get as close to that as possible.

Future – These clients/candidates fall into your prospect list. Use your existing connections to glean information up front, research the client website, Google the candidate, check out relevant LinkedIn pages. Consider your approach. How will you be different to all the other mediocre excuses for 'Business Development'? Be aware that, certainly from the client side it typically takes between 5 and 12 'touches' to secure a sale. A 'touch' could be an email, a telephone call, or a face-to-face dialogue. It should be obvious to you that the better the quality of the 'touch' the more you reduce the amount required to get that business.

From the candidate's perspective, well they want relevant 'touches' too. Speak their language, make their business *your* business and discuss relevant roles with them. As a recruitment 'breed' we are branded crap listeners, throwing out irrelevant roles to candidates and damaging our own credibility as well as that of our company and our industry. You've heard me refer to the importance of really understanding the key fundamentals of the sector you are working in. This is just one reason as to why it's so important.

Once you've mapped your client and candidate lists into your three categories of past, present, future, you now need to consider how many clients you have in total. If you have too few then you haven't scoped your market thoroughly enough. If you have too many then you're never going to get around them all thoroughly and that'll damage your conversion rates possibly beyond repair. Notice I'm not committing to stating what makes a sensible amount of clients. That will depend on your market sector as well as your own organisational skills as you need to be able to contact them all regularly.

Consider the candidates you have within your talent pool. Where are the shortages? Ask yourself if there are few of a particular type of candidate as there is little demand for those skills, experience or qualifications. If so, then don't waste your time in sourcing more. On the other hand, if the candidates that the market *does* want are those you don't have, then make a plan to find them! Those are the types of candidates to have on your radar, the proverbial rocking horse shit. Consider an attraction strategy that is enticing and truthful. No bullshit fake adverts please.

The frequency with which you contact your clients and candidates will vary based on request and circumstance, but typically 2-4 week rotations keep you sufficiently remembered without becoming a nuisance. Only as long as the quality and relevance of your contact is apparent in the communication though. Mix up your correspondence so it becomes a mixture of canvassing and adding value. Send out surveys, market information, business reports and any other sector-relevant literature. Give your candidates and clients what they want and they will remember you.

Use your Career Purpose to kick you up the bum and make this happen. Segment the project by setting SMARTASS goals for yourself and, finally make a Step Plan for the short-term tasks you need to do on a daily basis.

Let's get you started with some reflection space:

Note the name of one Past client and one Past candidate

_____

_____

_____

_____

_____

Now the name of one Present client and one Present candidate

_____

_____

_____

_____

_____

Now the name of one Future client and one Future candidate

_____

_____

_____

_____

_____

THE SMARTASS RECRUITER

Note down one Competitor you'll commit to researching

_____

_____

_____

_____

_____

And finally, note the names of some of your key colleagues, together with the role they have.

_____

_____

_____

_____

_____

Marketing basics

"To stay motivated you must be working for a purpose. Make sure every day you make a difference."

Billy Cox

As a recruitment consultant, you'll understand the importance of quality sales calls (or BD as its often labelled, standing for business development). If you don't then I'll discuss it with you later. But there's much more to how you market yourself than just BD. Everything you write and say to the outside world is a reflection of you and your brand, so choose your words wisely.

Let's take Social Media first – whether it's LinkedIn, Facebook or Twitter, if you are using your social media pages for business, be careful about how your profile looks, about what you post and about how you contribute to the posts of others. A selfie with a pint, a pout, your friends, your cleavage, your dog (cute as it might be), really doesn't cut it in the business world. At least not if you want to be taken seriously as a professional. Be provocative if you choose (in your post themes, not your dress code) but not unethical. Be controversial if you must but be careful of alienating or offending your network.

My advice; keep it industry related, topical, light-hearted & friendly. Contribute to similar posts by people in your network and make a point of liking and commenting on posts written by people on your target lists – but only if you have something relevant/intelligent to say! You should use the opportunity to demonstrate your market knowledge, rather than a lame "great post" remark which comes across cheesy, slightly desperate and adds no value. Sometimes less is more.

Be careful with your use of emojis, LOLs, kisses and the like; know your audience and remind yourself you are using this in a professional capacity. PMSL, WTF and OMFG should be kept for your own personal page IMHO (see what I did there). If in doubt on what is appropriate to post, then ask yourself whether your CEO would be happy to read it. If not, then you have your answer...

Your LinkedIn profile in particular should act as the window to your professional soul. Alongside your photograph, be sure to maximise the opportunities LinkedIn offers it's users. Become visible in the relevant circles for your industry sector. Follow prominent people such as business leaders, sector experts and any recruitment experts that you believe could either support you or who you could potentially support.

Ensure that your profile is complete. You simply must have a (professional) photograph on your profile page, as other users consider those LinkedIn members without less trustworthy. Be sure that your profile works to sell both who you are as well as the service you provide. Have your work history comprehensive and up to date, your education history complete (together with any additional development you have undertaken post-mainstream education) and also include any charities you may support or volunteering work you engage in. LinkedIn is a clever little so and so and prompts you to complete your profile. On the home page it'll highlight for you just how complete your profile is and suggest ways you can enhance it.

Add skills you have that so that others can endorse you. Ask to be recommended too (recommendations are different to endorsements) as recommendations are really beneficial. They act as social proof that you can, in fact, do what you say you can. They are extremely useful when it comes to demonstrating your service to potential candidates and clients. They don't just have to take your word for how good you are; instead they can view what others say about you. That's really powerful in business. However, do be careful about 'tit for tat' recommendations, i.e. I'll recommend you if you recommend me. Viewers of your profile can see whom you have given recommendations to and who has recommended you. If they match like for like, it all appears rather insincere and contrived. Or as I prefer to call them: bullshit referrals.

Join some groups. While I'm no LinkedIn expert I do know that on a free profile it's possible to join up to 50 different groups. So that means that, if you or your employer have a paid LinkedIn account, you may have access to more. There are recruiter groups, industry groups, and niche groups. It's down to you to choose the groups that you feel would be most relevant to your work and your network. The great thing about groups is that, once you've joined one, you can see all the members of that group. Furthermore this means that, if you choose to connect with any of them, you have a legitimate connection to them (you are members of the same group). It proves a very useful way to expand your network with relevant connections.

Finally, whenever you invite someone to connect, send a personalised message. It always goes down better than the default standard invite and allows you to stand out right from the start, for the right reasons.

Next let's think about emails. I mentioned earlier about the reputation recruiters have. It's important to be sure the right audience receives the relevant messages. Almost all recruitment database systems these days have the facility to mail merge without the need for a Masters degree in IT. Create several mailing lists if you need, but take the time to do it well. I'm all for making candidates and clients flexible, but let's not confuse that with sending out the completely wrong message on a whim and hoping for the best. That destroys the credibility of you and your company, often irreversibly.

Finally, the good old online Job Advert. Don't get me started on the absolute dross that adorns my screen so frequently as I scroll through my LinkedIn account (I keep scrolling by the way; 1, I'm not looking for a job, 2, rarely does anything catch my eye enough to even bother stopping). Endless reams of " I'm currently recruiting for…" "I have a great opportunity for…" all the way to the bottom of the barrel "(link to job description here)".

I do appreciate that there will be readers from across the recruitment spectrum and your advert style must match your market. But you really should think about what will make your advert different and eye-catching to prevent the continued scrolling of the candidates you need. Consider the candidates you want to attract – desperate die hard 'will apply for anything' types, immediately available or passive candidates. Trust me, the response you receive will be a direct reflection of your advertising style, so think carefully. Ask yourself what candidates actually look for; progression, autonomy, package, status, job security and so on. Tailor your advert to them and their needs, not you and yours. Speak their language. Make your advert stand out to candidates, pose a question or write a striking statement to grab attention, such as, "Still working extra hours to receive that ever-elusive promotion?" or "You can't have work/life balance and a good salary". Use more 'you' than 'I' in your advertising. Let me illustrate with a couple of simple examples:

Example A

I'm currently recruiting for an experienced Sales Recruiter to join us at Blahblah.

We are the fastest growing, biggest, most fabulous recruitment company in the world, consistently voted the best company to work for (you get the picture)

What we're looking for:

Proven Sales Ability
Tenacity
Drive and determination
A team player
Excellent communication skills

We offer flexible working hours and a competitive salary

Example B

You can't have work/life balance and a good salary

Is that what you're still being told? If you want to succeed in recruitment then you have to put in at least 50 hours a week, right?

How would you like to prove that wrong? How would you like to enjoy flexible working without compromising your finances?

You already have:

Proven Sales Ability
Tenacity
Drive and determination

Then you should come and join us at Blahblah as a Sales Recruiter. We are the fastest growing, biggest, most fabulous recruitment company in the world, consistently voted the best company to work for...

Did you see the difference? Hear the difference? Most importantly did you *feel* the difference? Please don't get me wrong, these are still not finished articles when it comes to advert writing (I'm not doing everything for you!!) but notice how simply flipping the language and appealing to those needs that you believe your readers are likely to have, instantly makes the advert more eye-catching and interesting. Your advert should be selling the experience, selling the dream and that's why you should be appealing to the emotions of your audience. Just like recruitment itself you are selling. Put yourself in the shoes of the candidate – are they really going to entrust their future to someone who can't be arsed to invest time in their advert writing? Are they going to trust that a recruiter who writes crap adverts can sell them into their dream employer? Unlikely.

Final rant – proofread and spell check. In today's world of gadgets and technology, there is simply no excuse for poor grammar and incorrect spelling.

If you still remain unconvinced, then Google 'best job adverts examples' and see what you find. If you don't see a style that resembles your own, then maybe it's time to change your style.

The Key to Successful Sales

"If you think you're too small to have an impact, try going to bed with a mosquito in the room."

Anita Roddick

I'm devoting a lengthy chapter to this as sales talent plays a huge part in the success of a Recruitment Consultant. Of course, everything you do, write and say with stakeholders is an opportunity to sell yourself and your company (hence my previous comments on advert writing), but in this chapter we're talking about getting on that BD bus. Hitting the phones and building relationships, working our way through our target lists to finally secure us some cash.

If you've gotten this far through the book, it tells me you weren't offended by my candid slating of some of the processes you currently adopt and that, ultimately you want to do more in your role as a recruitment consultant to succeed, great! Because this chapter will not only slate you all over again, but will also quite possibly be the most helpful of them all in your day-to-day sales activity.

Assuming you have categorised your target clients and you have created some great adverts to attract some relevant candidates, you should start by thinking about what other preparation to do before you dial out. Most importantly, what is the reason for your call? What is it you'd like to achieve? What information do you want to come away with? All too often, recruitment consultants start 'banging' the phones during power hour, core time, blitz - whatever you choose to call it – with no real clue as to why. Of course you want to get jobs and place candidates. But there's much more to it than that.

You need to be a business professional here and really give some thought as to what information will help you secure the right jobs and place the best candidates. Without preparing some objectives beforehand, you'll come across as just another uninspiring recruitment consultant asking the bog standard list of client questions, beginning with "are you recruiting at the moment?" and of candidates, "are you looking at the moment?' You'll also find yourself stumbling with everything that comes next, having no clear structure as to where you want to take the conversation. I've even heard recruiters get tongue tied when the answer to the question is "yes".

A recruitment consultant has the opportunity to write his or her own pay cheque. I know that's cheesy but it's true. But it doesn't just happen. It takes planning and execution. Planning doesn't have to take hours. I've met plenty of recruiters who've allegedly been planning when actually they are shuffling nervously to avoid making any real calls.

A few minutes well spent reviewing your existing database information, CV, websites and LinkedIn pages should suffice. The point of planning is to give you the structure to execute so be sure to do this. Oh and make sure you have a pen and paper at the ready. Don't underestimate the basics.

Now let's execute;

I am not (thankfully) a client or candidate in receipt of the tens of calls a day which begin with, "I'm just giving you a quick call to introduce myself as the new contact for your area" but there are many of them out there. Now you might be laughing at this because you know that's you, or you might be laughing at it because you know others who say it, or you might be laughing because at some point in the past, when you were a candidate or client, a recruitment consultant said it to you. Either way you're laughing.

You shouldn't be laughing
Your clients and candidates are not laughing

You should be cringing

Your clients and candidates are cringing

You should be mortified to think there are still hundreds; yes hundreds of Recruitment Consultants who still do this.

If you are one of them, stop. Right. Now. You sound like a twat, fact.

More than that, you crush any hope of sounding credible and promoting yourself as any kind of expert.

Allow me to translate my interpretation of "I'm just giving you a quick call to introduce myself as the new contact for your area".

"I lack confidence, I'm not giving any value with this call, I don't know what to say, I'm just the same as all the others, I have no idea what to ask you, I don't know what I can offer you, I'm probably new and therefore have no clue what I'm talking about, another member of our team has left, we can't keep our staff, I'm a twat".

While I appreciate that lot may not be what you intend to mean with such a feeble introduction, trust me; that's how it comes over. It's no surprise that often you won't even get past a receptionist or other gatekeeper. We'll talk more about this in the next chapter.

Every bit of sales training in the land will tell you to have a "hook". A reason for calling that engages your client or candidate to take an interest in your call and talk to you. Tell me, if you're intending to develop business through this call (that's why we call it BD!) then is your call really going to be that 'quick'. Seriously is 'introducing yourself' really the best you can do as a reason for calling?

And that's why every consultant's start point has to be in the planning phase. If you've formulated your target list suitably into your past, present and future lists then that's certainly a great help for client calls. It'll help you in deciding what you want to get from each call (your objectives) and will allow you to plan your hook and the structure of your call. If you haven't, go back and read it again and do that first – mark this page and come back to it.

Assuming you now have some initial structure, use this to help create your hook. We'll focus on clients first. A hook needs to be something of interest to them, something that benefits them, like a hot candidate (hot off the press, not great-looking), a relevant piece of marketing, a topical white paper or informing them of new legislation; ideally also something that differentiates you from all the other callers.

Referring to your hook early in the call won't guarantee they will talk to you (they may genuinely be busy), but it'll give you a whole lot better a chance than saying "I'm just giving you a quick call to introduce myself as the new contact for your area"

A few extra points worth noting here too.

The first is that one of my (and many peoples) pet hates is being asked the question, "How are you today?" by someone I've never spoken to before. In fact I find it rather offensive and when it happens to me, the caller is then on the back foot as I'm just waiting to smash them out of the water and tell them to piss off. Call me harsh but I'm not alone in this. I appreciate it's said –in the most part – with positive intention, but it comes over more often than not as condescending and insincere. Not the traits I'm looking for in my recruitment consultant of choice.

The second is that, regardless of how many calls you make you will undoubtedly fall foul of the dreaded voicemail. The majority either hangs up there and then and proceeds to fake it as a sales call on the internal system, or at best you leave your name and number and hope they call back. Chances are that in 99% of cases they won't return your call. So leave you hook as part of the message and tell them you'll try again. At least give yourself the best shot here. Again, it won't guarantee a response, but you've given yourself permission to call again – and that creates your next hook – win: win.

Thirdly, I referred earlier to the fact that there should be very little actual 'cold calling' in recruitment and the reasons are, that out of your target lists only your future clients will fall into the cold call category. It may also transpire that someone else from your company has called in the past, which means they are not, strictly speaking, cold. From the few that remain, those will be as cold as you let them be. If you've done your research on the client via their website, their LinkedIn page and Google, then you should have an insight into them. The more insight you have, the warmer that makes the call as you can refer to that research when you speak with them.

I take the point I may be stretching this a little here. There are indeed some tough cookies out there, some with apparent hearts of stone. Your job is to soften them. It's a big part of your role, so you should want to make it an area of focus.

The fourth point is that everything I'm referring to also applies to candidates. They *too* want to hear your hook, something you have of value for them, and a reason for calling that makes you stand out and makes you different. Don't forget that if you want to get them on side early right from the outset.

Remember to plan call times. Simple but important. Monday mornings and Friday afternoons were the worst times for me to ever have success with either candidates or clients. Sunday was often one of the most effective days to post social media comments or private message (when there were no 'work' distractions). Another reason to know your market. If it's typical for your networks to be off-site by lunchtime on a Thursday, then use that information when you plan your call times. In the finance arena, month end was a big no-go for calling clients and candidates. Work with your market, not against it.

My final point; be sure to align your greeting to that of your audience. Especially on your initial call to a client remind yourself that you are the professional. 'Hiya' doesn't sit well with me; and you are certainly not their 'mate' or 'pal' at this stage of your relationship, so don't refer to them as such. You may not need to be as formal as 'Mr Smith' for instance, but over-familiarity will be a sure fire way of pissing a whole load of potential customers off before you've even begun.

So I called this chapter The Key to Successful Sales and although all of the above is useful and extremely important, I haven't yet referred to my 'key'.

So here it is:

The key to successful sales is the ability to ask intelligent questions.

Read that again and really take it in. Emphasise the word *intelligent* as you read.

Planning is crucial, a hook that engages the client or candidate could make the difference between having a conversation and not.

Handy Hint

Intelligent questions – lots of them – are the key ingredient to successful sales.

Fundamentally in sales, you are a problem solver. Does that sound unrealistic? Hear me out on this. Almost every sales book in the world will suggest that in order to sell your product or service to an end user, you simply have to understand what they need from you. After that, well then it's about establishing whether you can give them what they need.

So, find out what they need and give them the solution. Solve the problem. Now the problem in itself might not be as tangible as "we need a candidate with 'x' skillset" or "I'm looking for "x" role". It's often more than that, much more. On the client side, consider what the client's vision (or purpose) is and how their strategy leads to its fulfilment. Then you not only get a deeper sense of the wider recruitment need, but also you know more about the client to pass on to candidates and colleagues in your organisation. The same principles apply on the candidate side too. Knowing the wider Career Purpose of the candidate gives you much more insight to match the right role/client fit for them in fulfilling that.

The single biggest problem I see across the recruiting industry is a distinct lack of deep questioning.

Just for a minute, imagine you are the candidate. As a recruitment consultant I could find lots of potential roles and organisations for you to work within, agreed?

I ask you questions around your location, skills, qualifications, salary expectation and so on. Those questions filter at one level. I now know that you won't be suited to a certain number of companies based upon those criteria.

We continue on with questions about your motivators. You perhaps give me an answer to this around progression, training, recognition etc. Great, I can now filter further, but you'll agree there are still a lot of companies who would still be able to meet these criteria.

In many ways that's a good thing; I have lots of companies I can market you in to and chances are you'll get invited to interview with some. You might even get a job offer. Let's assume you do.

Some companies offer these 'meet the team' soirees as part of the latter stages of the interview process. You know the sort, where you all chat and get the low down on the team (and they on you), you hear a bit more schmooze about how great it is to work at the company and you're even more committed to joining.

And sometimes that's good enough. Sometimes you'll have a long term match made in heaven.

And sometimes it's not good enough. Sometimes you'll join that company and shortly after the honeymoon period is

over you'll realise that something isn't quite right; some of the people you had such fun with at your soiree turn out to be dirty snakes in the grass who'd sell you down the river to protect their own asses. There are things about the company; practices, processes, people, that just give you that uncomfortable feeling. For a while – maybe 12-18 months if you're lucky - you roll with it for the sake of your CV. You become one of the moaners for a while; you even become one of the schmoozers at the soiree with the next poor bastards excited at the prospect of joining your company. "Maybe if more people come on board things will change" you tell yourself, "maybe if I get that promotion", "maybe if my manager leaves". Your life becomes a series of maybes. But nothing changes and eventually you're knocking on your recruiter's door again with a bullshit reason for leaving such as 'I'm ready for a new challenge'.

Most of us have been *that* candidate at some point in our career. If you haven't yet then you might be there now. Or be aware it could be yet to come.

You get the picture.

Is there really anything more recruitment consultants can ask of candidates to help break this cycle of stress and dissatisfaction? A deeper level of questioning would undoubtedly help and we'll cover more of this shortly, but how often do we ask candidates about the Values they hold dear and their wider Career Purpose – their 'why'? Rarely I'd suspect. Sounds too fluffy doesn't it? Yet it's so important we understand this, as it's often a misalignment with core Values and Career Purpose that creates the discord in our working relationships. The things that sometimes, we can't put our finger on yet we know something 'just doesn't feel right'.

This will be the greatest 'need' any candidate has in a long-term temporary role or in a permanent role. To be granted the opportunities to fulfil that Career Purpose in an organisation that aligns with their personal Values. That's what you'd want.

Notice how this filters in a way like no other. You now have a differentiated, yet absolutely sincere reason to present them to your client as the best fit for the role and the organisation.

To be clear, establishing Values and Career Purpose does not replace the need for the other questions, but it complements them beautifully.

Now let's return to your client questioning technique. Ask yourself what types of questions you currently ask your clients. Probably some fairly superficial level questions in many cases; are you recruiting? Do you use agencies? Where are you based? I'm not trying to insult anyone's intelligence here. There are probably other questions you ask too. The point I'm making is that recruitment consultants are so keen to 'flog in' their candidate and so keen to get off the phone to make the next call (such is your KPI-driven life), that 9 times out of 10 the amount of questions asked can be counted on one hand.

Going back to complete basics here —my experience and research tells me that rapport building is easy for recruiters. Generally you're a nice bunch. But *nice* on its own won't cut it in business.

I said the key to successful sales is the ability to ask *intelligent* questions. Stupid ones won't get you far.

I remind you that you are probably one of 5, 10, 20 other recruitment consultants to have called them that week (in some cases that day!) Clients are actually sick of hearing same old same old questions. They know the drill and sometimes they play the game. But sometimes they don't. Your job is to control the conversation flow, rather than be controlled. I rarely accept that clients 'just won't give any information'. I translate that as 'I asked stupid questions'.

THE SMARTASS RECRUITER

Sorry, but you know I'm right.

As a consultant you should be acting as an expert.
Sometimes expertise takes time. That's why taking time
out to really understand your market is so important.

How often do you ask questions about the client's business
strategy, the plans they have for the organisation over the
next 12 months? (I mean generally, NOT just related to
recruitment opportunities). How often do you ask what the
Values of the clients business are and how they would
expect personnel to demonstrate these in their work? How
often do you ask what they like about their current
recruitment methods, rather than only what is missing?

The most successful recruiters will show a genuine interest
in the overall client situation. They will know that a
recruitment career is a marathon and not a sprint. They
will know that asking
intelligent questions
shortens the sales
cycle and ultimately
increases their own
standard of living,
feeling of wellbeing and leave them less stressed. It also
brings them closer to fulfilling their Career Purpose.

You may remember I mentioned earlier that there are some suggestions that going from completely cold with a client through to securing a sale takes between 5 & 12 'touches'. Remember that a touch point could be an email, a phone call, a meeting. The better you investigate with intelligent questions, the fewer the touches you'll need. If you're taking 12 touches or more to secure business, then you've either categorised your client incorrectly in your planning phase or you're not asking enough intelligent questions – simple.

Of course, no matter how many questions you ask, if you don't uncover any issues then you still have nothing to sell to. No problem identified, no solution needed. But let's be positive about this and assume your Career Purpose is so clear and your SMARTASS goal so aligned that you do uncover something.

So when you hear of any kind of need, challenge or problem, make sure you grab that, focus on the negative effect that need must be having on the client, their team, their project etc. and solve that (if you can). There's no point missing this completely and suggesting you'll send some details on an email or you'll call back next week. That problem is a massive buying signal for a recruiter. It might be a lack of skilled candidates, candidates that don't turn up, an unreliable current provider etc. That's your "in"; you now need to know if you can solve it.

I've worked with consultants who lie, blatantly. Those who think it's a great idea to say on the phone that they have the right 'skilled candidates' and then worry about finding them later. Now, I'm an advocate of demonstrating shrewd commercial acumen, but I'm very much *not* an advocate of bullshit. In my opinion, this example is the latter.

You may get lucky, you may actually find a candidate who is rarer than rocking horse shit. But it's unlikely and will just leave you looking like the bullshitter you are. Furthermore, you know that opportunity you just had? Well it's gone... probably forever.

It's precisely these kind of sneaky recruitment consultant tactics that bring the industry into disrepute. Please stop if you're an offender. Play the long game rather than the quick buck rodeo. Reputations take a long time to build and just moments to shatter!

Clients would much rather you were honest about things. In this example, tell them you know that those kind of candidates are scarce, find out what they would need, see if there's any flexibility (given the fact that not having that candidate will be probably having a detrimental effect on their business) and suggest you'll use your knowledge and your network to see how you can help.

So much better isn't it? You know it and clients know it.

As an added bonus you're more likely to get some added commitment from them in gratitude for your honesty – the chance to meet with them perhaps, a temporary worker to support in the interim.

Handy Hint

Play the long game...

Notice how the importance of your competitor knowledge also plays a vital role here. You may be thinking that these methods and this honesty is all well and good if you have a role exclusively, but not if you have your competitors working the role too. If you're playing the long game you'll realise that sometimes waiting for your competitors to fail and be exposed as bullshitters is the way to win the race. Know whom it is you're up against and how they would likely behave in a given scenario. In sport they say the key is all about studying the habits of your opponents, so much so that you can anticipate their next move, all the time ready to thwart their attempts. In business, the same principles apply. Be aware and knowledgeable. If you're neither then how can you sensibly prepare for the counter?

Just as with every part of this book, I'm focusing on candidates as well as clients.

Find out what they like about their current role or their previous role as well as what is missing for them. Once you've uncovered what they want/need and are not getting from their current role/manager/company, then that's the 'problem' you have to solve. Bridge the gap. In just the same way, be honest. If you can't help them then tell them. Don't keep the poor sods hanging from a thread, sitting by the phone expecting a call from you that's never going to come through. In the next chapter we'll discuss candidate care in more detail. Honest feedback; frankly *any* feedback – or rather the lack thereof – from recruitment consultants, is one of the many rants I see on social media over and over again. Now consistency is important, as long as it's not crap. Candidates of today are often the clients of tomorrow. Don't screw up your pipeline.

Now, let's assume you've done everything well. You've asked great questions and uncovered a buying signal, a problem, and a need. It may not give you immediate results but you still have a 'bite' and you need to ensure you don't lose it. As an aside, I think in all my years in recruitment I only ever picked up a booking on my first call to a new, completely cold client, on a handful of occasions. And let's look at that in more detail; if I can pick up a client in 1 call, then my competitor can steal them from me in 1 call. In other words, that client (or candidate, as the same principles apply here) isn't likely to have any real loyalty to me or any agency for that matter. I actually *like* the fact I need to work a bit, the thrill of the chase I guess. The wooing of the potential client or candidate until finally they succumb to your charms. (In a truly professional sense, naturally). That's how you build relationships for the long term. I say again, you should be playing the long game.

So back to your buying signal – make sure you offer a potential solution. This is where the knowledge you should have about your own company and the services you offer kicks in. This is where you may be tested about how you compare with other agencies too, so be sure you have done your competitor research.

And be sure to offer a potential solution that is relevant. There is no point listing off a series of things you offer if none of them match what the client needs. So offer something relevant and be sure to articulate how your potential solution solves their unique problem and also how it solves the effect the problem has on them and their business. Make it personal rather than a corporate list. Frankly the client doesn't give a shit if your company has a huge database of candidates (for instance). Selfishly perhaps, but all they want to know is how that solves their problem. It's your job to tell them that clearly.

Assuming you have offered a relevant potential solution, test how that feels for the client. Ensure that they are on board with you before you finish your call. And regardless whether you just secured a role to work on or whether you have simply generated some interest in future use, get something of value before you close your call. With clients, consider the thing that gets you closest to the sale that is acceptable to ask for. An immediate start – that's closest to the sale. Sending an email – that's the furthest away.

Everything in between consists of securing an interview, sending a CV, canvassing a Job on, arranging a meeting, a call back etc. You know the drill.

With candidates, gain agreement for a job start, attending an interview, gain their commitment to be submitted for a role or at very least arrange a meeting to register them in person.

There are some great quotes out there about reaching for the moon and landing among the stars. And, other than the occasional social media meme you upload and possible framed poster of it adorning the wall of your home or your office, that's generally as much as that comes to life. Why oh why do so many recruitment consultants feel it's good practise to simply say they will send an email to clients and say to candidates you'll 'bear them in mind' – with zero attempt at even asking for anything more?

Often the reasons are related back to the beginning of this BD process, in setting out your objectives. If you never really had a reason to call (2-3 reasons ideally so you have your back up objectives) other than getting a job/availability, then when you realise there isn't a job/availability to get you have nothing more to consider.

I think that, regardless of whether the client is recruiting or not, if there is a future opportunity you should at very least be asking to meet. And if they're not recruiting at the moment so much the better. They have more time to meet you while they aren't in the throes of ploughing through a sea of CVs. Give them a reason to meet you that benefits them.

Please for the love of god do not suggest 'putting a face to a name'. This is another of my massive pet hates. I mean, what the actual fuck does that phrase mean? In today's world, anyone can click on your LinkedIn profile and 'voila' a face is put to a name. No meeting necessary. It's another feeble excuse which translates (in my world) as 'I have no idea what I'm going to say to you in the meeting', 'I have nothing of value to offer you', 'I'm hoping by some magical intervention you'll give me all your future business' and my personal favourite, 'I have my KPIs to hit'

Do you now see how poor that sounds? Do not say it. Ever.

Instead, think about all those legitimate reasons you could give; discuss future recruitment and company strategy, find out more about what they look for in a recruitment partner, visit the premises to understand the culture and so on. Much better. Much more credible. Much more 'consultant'.

There are some suggestions that when we give the human brain a choice, it makes one. Tea or coffee? Red or blue? 2 or 3 o'clock? I'm not certain whether any research actually backs this theory, but it makes sense and certainly in my experience I've found this method of closing to be particularly effective. Known as the 'alternative close', it allows the closer to manipulate the response according to his/her own constraints and capability. If you know that Monday and Friday are no go days for you to go to meetings, then offer to come over Tuesday or Wednesday instead. Let's pretend they choose Tuesday. You can now look at your diary and suggest times that suit your schedule. Perhaps I have another meeting in the morning, so I offer 3.30 or 4.30pm. They choose 4.30pm and the meeting is set.

If you search for 'closing techniques' on the World Wide Web there are literally hundreds – some better than others. The alternative close is my particular favourite, because although you are controlling the schedule, the client or candidate feels as though they are in control, and that's how everyone likes to feel.

If you're unable to close for some reason, chances are you aren't offering enough value to warrant that commitment. Or maybe, once again, you just didn't ask enough intelligent questions.

Final thought:

Handy Hint

If you don't ask, you don't get

So ask questions and ask for some form of commitment on *every* call you make.

It's been a long old chapter (I said it would be lengthy) and it's one I could have gone on with for much longer. Allow me to summarise before offering you an opportunity to capture your thoughts.

Have a strategy. Do your research and decide what you want to achieve from the call. 2-3 objectives are recommended. Aim high!

Have a hook. A reason for calling that benefits your recipient. Prepare this prior to calling.

Ask lots of intelligent questions! Not just about recruitment but about the 'Values' of your client/candidate and longer-term strategies. Really get to know them. Simple tip that's often forgotten – What, Who, Why, Where, When, How, are all 'open' questions so be sure to ask more of them in order to get your client/candidate talking.

Find out what's missing. What isn't your client getting from their current recruitment methods? What's missing from your candidate's role that stops it being their perfect job?

Find out how much that hurts! What impact does 'what's missing' have on them personally, as a team/family, as an organisation?

Ensure you can solve the problem – know your offering AND your competitors offering so you can truly oversell.

Highlight how solving the problem has a positive impact on what's hurting!

Ask for something! Close them by gaining some commitment – again, aim high but recognise you are playing the long game so don't expect all the business without needing to work for it.

Ok so now over to you. Take some notes and come back to this often – it's a major step in changing your sales results for the better!

What reasons could I give for calling a client that benefits them?

And how about a candidate?

List some 'open' questions you could hear yourself using.
Pay attention to those that look to identify challenges or
needs and remember to build the issue through asking
questions around the impact of the challenge

Note some common responses to 'what's missing?' from
clients

And from candidates

List as many things as you can that you and your company can offer to solve this

And finally, research some closing techniques from the internet and choose some you like

To me, to you

"Let us never negotiate out of fear. But never fear to negotiate."

John F. Kennedy

Have you ever negotiated yourself a discount anywhere? You have? It feels good doesn't it? If you haven't then you really should try it. The next time you're booking a holiday or perhaps the next time you broker a deal on a car. Something as big as a house purchase or as little as a toaster, be sure to ask what discounts are available. You'd be surprised at how frequently you'll receive a discount or a freebie. Granted, the retailer will probably want something in return. Perhaps a discount would be given on a holiday if you take foreign currency from the travel agent. Take GAP insurance on your car and you might get yourself a deal on price. House buyers usually negotiate discounts if they can move quickly or have no chain and you could potentially get yourself a free toaster the next time you buy your next smart TV.

What you'll also find is that, in many cases, the seller is *expecting* you to ask. In fact they often wait for you to start the bartering process. So expected is the haggling that prices are often inflated slightly to allow for negotiation.

The important part to a successful negotiation is that you

get the discount you want (or at least some of it) and the seller gets the commitment from you that they want (or some of it) and secures the sale. It provides a 'win-win' outcome as everyone leaves feeling happy.

Negotiation isn't just reserved for the high street though. It's also an important part of the recruitment process. Furthermore, you should expect to have to negotiate as your clients and candidates certainly will want to in most cases.

To be clear, what negotiation *isn't* is simply dropping your fee, or giving a discount on price to your clients. It isn't just sacrificing your profit margin to give your candidate an extra few pence an hour. The technical term for what that is, is 'dropping your pants'. Giving something away without getting something else back from your client or your candidate is foolish and definitely not commercial best practise. You'll find yourself working hard rather than smart and that promotion, pay rise and top position on the league table will find itself increasingly elusive.

The first thing to be aware of is to *expect* to negotiate. Just like those retailers, you should anticipate the need to negotiate before the need actually arises. Let's face it, if you were a client using a recruitment consultant wouldn't you push your luck a bit and ask for a discount or extended payment terms? I would. If you were a candidate securing your next role, wouldn't you try and secure yourself the highest amount of money possible? I would.

The problem is that when they get asked, recruiters take it personally. Do they not realise how hard I've worked on this! Do they not want me to earn any commission! Bastards! And as soon as you take it personally, you lose focus of how to deal with the situation. Instead, remind yourself it's not personal. Most of the time *you* are not that important to be honest. Sorry to be the bearer of such devastating news but this is business and negotiation happens in business. Get over yourself and get yourself equipped to know what you want to ask of your clients and candidates in return for what they want.

The second thing to be aware of is the more you know what things you have to play with (give away and ask for in return), the better the negotiation will be. This isn't the time to be hesitating and tripping over your words. That just makes you sound like an arse to be honest. Be clear on what you will and will not move on. Be clear on what you are and are not authorised to give away. Be clear on exactly what stage you are happy to walk away from the deal. Deliver your message confidently and professionally.

The third thing to be aware of is to know what's really important to your client or candidate. Negotiation doesn't have to just be about money. It might be that your client will pay you a full fee *if* they can spread their payments. A discount won't make a whole lot of difference to them if that isn't really what's important. So don't rush to drop your pants on price. It might not get you anywhere and you'll end up bare-arsed and still without that deal sewn up. It might be that your temp candidate really needs long term work so will look to sting you on a pay rate for short term roles. Find them more stable work and you no longer need to drop your pants on pay rates. Perhaps that permanent candidate who seems inflexible, who is demanding a higher salary than the market dictates, really needs a pension scheme. Instead of to-ing and fro-ing over money, all you have to do is find a role with a pension. Stop assuming the most important thing to clients and candidates is always money. It isn't. Your job is to find out, in advance, exactly what makes them tick. Then you'll be in a far better position to get successful outcomes. For you and for them.

Negotiation is a crucial skill for a recruiter to have, yet still so many of you rush to drop your pants and give away money. I suggest you take some time to research exactly what you can ask for from your candidates and clients in return for discounts and pay changes, as well as the parts of your service you can take away. Feel free to use the space below to note all of it and ensure your pants remain firmly pulled up!

Talking of pay changes; when was the last time you increased *your* rates? You may laugh but I'm serious. I don't mean suddenly adding hundreds of pounds to your invoice values. I mean small, incremental increases of a few pence per hour and small 'pence per hour' deductions from temporary workers. Hear me out on this one.

Some rates are predetermined, I get that. Contracts and preferred supplier agreements dictate pay and charge rates for temporary workers and fee percentages for permanent workers. Some workers will be paid minimum wage so legally (and morally) you couldn't reduce this further.

This is not about shafting your candidates or your clients, but instead thinking commercially when you quote fees and pay rates.

How many of your current permanent placements are charged at your full rate? When you discount, what do you do? Discount the rate from 30% to 25%, from 25% to 20%? What about all the 'bits' in between? Have you ever discounted

30% to 28.5%? If you haven't, give some thought to how much additional revenue you would have made. On a 60k salaried role with a 30% fee, full billing would be £18000. Discounting this to 25% fee loses you £3000. Three grand you've just thrown away! Take the discount to 28.5% and you give away £900. Quite a difference hey.

But what happens if your clients are dissatisfied with that?

Here's an alternative; take the discount off the invoice value, rather than your fee percentages. Giving a 5% discount (the equivalent of the earlier example) off the invoice value means 5% off £18000 and that's your modest £900 discount. Sounds like a bigger discount but actually isn't.

Still be sure to get something back in return of course. Otherwise you're back to pant dropping.

Now to your temporary rates. How many of your charge rates and pay rates end in a '0' or a '5'? Most of them I suspect. Why is that? Maybe that's what you've always done or what you've seen others do. But you want to work smarter not harder, right?

If a client would pay £21.00 per hour for a worker, then they would likely pay £21.19 per hour. And you just made another 19 pence per hour for every hour that candidate works. Furthermore, if your candidate would work for £16.00 per hour, the chances are they would work for £15.86 per hour. Another 14 pence in your pocket for every hour they work. Assuming this pay and charge example is for the same booking, you have just made an additional 33 pence per hour for every hour worked in that booking.

Over the course of a typical 40-hour week, that totals £13.20 additional revenue from that booking alone. Now multiply that by 10 bookings, 40 bookings, and 100 bookings. It soon adds up. It's not ripping anyone off; it's working commercially.

And all you have to do is ask!

Handy Hint

I was always taught
never to quote a
temporary rate ending in
a '0' or a '5' and it
made a big difference to
my billed revenue (and
my commission).
What difference would it
make to yours?

Let's reflect on that for a moment, while you consider your notes from this chapter.

What can I negotiate with for my clients?

What can I negotiate with for my candidates?

What will I do differently with my quotations?

Gatekeepers and other blockers

"Obstacles don't have to stop you. If you run into a wall don't turn around and give up. Figure out how to climb it, go through it, or work around it."

Michael Jordan

THE SMARTASS RECRUITER

We've covered the fundamentals to the sales and negotiation process. But as a recruitment consultant you need to be aware (if you aren't already) that life doesn't run that smoothly and almost always, you will encounter an obstacle somewhere on your journey. Especially when it comes to dealing with clients.

I get asked frequently what a consultant should do if they get blocked immediately by a client receptionist, other gatekeeper or even the decision maker themselves.

 I have a number of theories here and we'll go through them now.

My first theory (and this is hugely important) is that 9 out of 10 times you have brought this upon yourself. Introducing yourself as 'new' or using another equally shocking opener acts as an instant turn off to most clients. The receptionist or gatekeeper has heard it all before and will revel in getting rid of you as quickly as possible. And saying it to the decision maker is just recruiter suicide. If you read the last chapter you'll now know why.

Similarly if you're asking lots of uninspiring questions – probably mainly 'closed' questions (i.e. can only be answered 'yes' or 'no') that will undoubtedly lead you to the inevitable 'no' quickly. You are transparent to your clients and your methods are flawed. Essentially you are questioning them only for your own gain – Are you recruiting? Do you use agencies? Can I get the next opportunity? And so on. There's not a whole lot in it for them.

Think about going on a date. Typically we begin with questions about the other person's background don't we? The things they like and dislike, their hobbies etc. We both flatter them and we take an interest in them. It would be a bit odd to go straight in with questions like, do you like brown hair with blue eyes then? Have you slept with many people? Do you shag on a first date?

That approach will likely get you a slap round the face and certainly not the long-term result you'd like. So why would you think client relationships are any different. You are basically being too direct with your clients, with all one-way traffic, rushing the process and they are slapping you around the face. Quite right too!

Take heed of my advice on questioning – intelligent questions are the key to successful sales remember. Consider how your current questions could be walking you straight into a metaphorical slap over and over again.

Just like on a first date, flatter your client and genuinely take an interest in them and their business. Remember people love to talk about themselves, so get them talking and build some of this rapport recruitment consultants are supposedly great at.

Another theory I have is how dismissive we can be of the receptionist or gatekeeper when we call. Finding ourselves acting almost as if they are not a real person. We are so busy on our 'must get through to the decision maker' mission, that we forget a number of things about the person on the phone right now:

1. they *are* a real person. Treat them with the respect they deserve. That person is someone's mother/father, son/daughter. Be friendly, polite, get their name and thank them for their help – whatever the outcome.

2. they will sometimes have strict instructions not to put you through to the decision maker. That is not their fault

and they shouldn't be blamed. You just need to get more creative with your approach.

3. they are allowed to have a bad day. There is another great quote that I recall as, "Everyone is on a journey you know nothing about. Be kind, always". Enough said.

4. they can be a fantastic source of information! Chances are they know lots of the information you need to know about the business to build your company 'picture'. If it's a receptionist they see all the visitors, temporary workers and interviewees coming through the door. They will know the decision maker and be able to provide a valuable insight as to what they look for in a recruiter as well as what they are like as a person. Yet the best we usually come up with is, "when's a better time to call back?" Duh!

5. they probably start work later than you do, take a full lunch hour (lucky bastards) and finish before you do. So if all else fails, call again out of hours to bypass them

Another theory is that we expect a magic wand to help remove blockers. Frankly if someone stops you mid-flow and says a harsh, 'not interested', followed swiftly by hanging up the phone, I can't help you. My advice, call another time and try a different approach, get straight in with your hook before they can hang up, or send them something on email/in the post to pre-empt your call. It might warm them up a bit or it might not. That's sales for you.

If all this still isn't successful, then think a little further outside of the box. Email the DM (decision maker) in advance of your call. Try using their name more assertively (although don't be rude) i.e. 'John Smith please' or 'put me through to John Smith please'. When asked who's calling simply give your name, rather than you role and company name. If asked what the call is regarding, say simply, 'he'll know what it's regarding'. Well he will be expecting your call if you've emailed him previously!

Again, never be rude and please don't lie – you are NOT the hospital, his wife, his long lost cousin etc. That is stepping back on the bullshit bus and no one wants to ride on that.

Assuming you manage to either sidestep or breakthrough

the gatekeeper's rough exterior, I recognise that as a recruitment consultant, you will inevitably still receive some objections from client DMs themselves. I've heard everything from 'not recruiting' to 'we have a PSL' to 'you people are too expensive' and everything in between.

The first consideration is this. Which are saying 'I will not use you' and which are saying 'I cannot use you'? There's a distinct difference and one that you should probe further. I'll help you with that.

The vast majority of the blockers we receive are under the category of 'I cannot use you'.

My thoughts are that this actually translates to one of two things:

1, I don't *believe* I can use you

2, I can't use you *yet*.

Examples of what you might hear from a client which reflect these are:

We are not recruiting

We have a PSL (a preferred supplier list)

We advertise our roles

We recruit internally

We don't have the budget

So how do you deal with these? I'll firstly tell you what you don't do. You don't quit. None of this, 'ok then thanks for your time, bye' crap. If you're going be a successful recruiter you need to think on and embrace these objections as a key part of the sales process. Changing your mind-set about objections will help get you in the zone to challenge them (positively). You may not be surprised to hear me suggest you return to asking intelligent questions. Let's take each in turn:

We are not recruiting:

When did you last recruit?

What position was it for?

What methods did you use to recruit the role?

Which method was the most successful for you?

What challenges did you face?

How did the challenges impact you?

What would you have done differently if you had the time again?

What would you do next time you need to recruit?

We have a PSL:

What type of PSL is it? (There are loads of PSL types and each has a different implication for you – RPO (Recruitment Process Outsourcing), MSP (Managed Service Provider), Neutral Vendor, Master Vendor, Tiered PSL, Informal PSL)

What roles does the PSL cover? (It could be that the PSL doesn't even cover the staff you supply!)

What type of recruitment does the PSL cover? (temp/perm/both?)

How is the PSL performing?

What do you like about the PSL?

What were the reasons you chose the suppliers you did?

What are the most difficult positions to source?

What impact do these difficulties have on you?

What are the implications for you of recruiting outside of the PSL if those suppliers are struggling?

What is the tender process?

We advertise our roles:

What's the reason you choose that recruiting method?

How successful is this method?

Where do you advertise?

How do you reclaim back the cost of the advert?

How many responses do you typically get from each advert?

(If a lot of responses) How do you factor in the time to read and respond to them all?

(If only a few responses) What is your contingency plan?

What impact does a lot/few responses have on you?

How happy are you in paying fees in advance of securing the right candidate?

We recruit internally:

How successful is this method?

What do you like about managing the process internally?

How does your internal team market your requirements?

What are the positions that are most difficult to fill?

What are your contingency plans?

We don't have the budget:

What budget do you have?

How important is this role to you and your business?

How does the cost of recruiting compare with the cost of not having the right person in the role?

The remaining objections fall into the 'I will not use you' category and the only real ones here are:

1. We've had a bad experience with agencies
2. We've had a bad experience with you

These need even more empathy and probing, but without the rush to sell on. When trust is broken (whether the agency was yours or not), it takes time to rebuild. But if you're successfully able to 'woo' these clients back slowly and consistently, they will be loyal to you. Here are some of the questions worth asking in response to this blockers:

We've had a bad experience with agencies/with you:

What specifically happened?

What were you promised by that agency/us?

What did you expect from them/us that you didn't receive?

What aspects of the experience did go well?

How would you want an agency/us to demonstrate they/we would fulfil your expectations?

How are you now recruiting?

How successful is that?

Be careful about rushing to bad-mouth another employee at your company, whether they are currently employed by you or not. Like I mentioned in an earlier chapter, the client really (at this stage at least) will only see and hear your company name and will tar you all with the same 'incompetence brush'.

Ensure you react with empathy to this sort of blocker, especially if the bad experience was with your company. Excuses will not go down well and will only inflame the situation and the ill feeling your client may have. Instead, respond sincerely and genuinely. Really take time to listen to what your client wanted from their experience and what was missing to leave them feeling so disgruntled. It will serve you well.

Expect to make several calls to turn around a lapsed client like this. I said previously that you shouldn't be rushing in to sell at this point. It will likely have the opposite effect if you do and the client will be left feeling like your empathy was fake and you are more bothered about your sales targets than the service you provide. And you know where they will take those thoughts? Straight to a bloody recruiter bashing LinkedIn post!

The only others you may hear are those such as, 'I'm not interested' or (on a really bad day) 'get lost'. If you hear either of these, take some time to evaluate how engaging your original hook was. You will usually receive these fob-offs (they are not blockers) at the start of your call, so it just goes to highlight how important your call planning and execution is.

I think that's everything covered about handling the key blockers you may hear. Naturally there could be others that crop up, so give some thought to those and how you would question the client further in order to understand them in more detail.

If it's appropriate then offer a relevant solution to the need that you have uncovered and continue your call structure as before, concluding by gaining some form of commitment as you wrap up.

Handy Hint

The final thing to
remember is that the
majority of the blockers
that can be worked
through will happen
during the questioning
phase of your call.
So remember to return to
that once you've dealt
with the objection.

Scripted calls are dull and obviously scripted, structured calls are useful and provide a call 'bookmark' so you stay on track. But first and foremost you are having conversations and that means you can be taken off track frequently. Listen, take notes, engage and respond appropriately, returning to your structure, as it's relevant. Oh and the more conversations you have, the easier it becomes – and the more chance you'll keep your job and secure some great results.

Remind yourself of your Career Purpose, reflect on your SMARTASS goals and recognise the correlation between moving through blockers to achieving your goals.

Consider some of the common objections you receive on your calls and ask yourself:

_____

_____

_____

_____

_____

What can I do differently in my calls that will help minimise some of these blockers in the first place?

_____

_____

_____

_____

_____

What are some of the questions I will use in order to get past blockers in the future?

_____

_____

_____

_____

_____

Why life would be easier without Candidates

"Either you run the day, or the day runs you..."

Jim Rohn

I reflected on this a lot during my operational career – if only I didn't have to deal with candidates then this job would be so much easier.

Ring any bells?

They don't turn up when they say they will, they change their minds, they accept other jobs at the last minute, they disappear off the radar, they let me down at interview, they let me down at work, they lie. And then they have the cheek to criticise recruitment consultants! Basically they are a fucking nightmare and you could do without them.

If you've worked in recruitment for a while, you'll get where I'm coming from. If you're new to this, then I'm pre-warning you. You probably went into this industry (ultimately) to make a difference to your life and to the lives of others (even though you said you were 'target-driven' at your interview). Yet before long you begin to loathe people and their incessant ever-changing personalities. You become sceptical of them, untrusting and eventually uncaring. As the KPI-reaper creeps ever closer month after month, you care less and less.

Now I'm not actually suggesting that you are an uncaring, sociopathic monster (but if the cap fits?). I'm merely suggesting that the longer a career in recruitment goes on, the more you tend to lose the personal touch. Even the internal language used in organisations is about 'bookings filled' and 'placements'. The candidate as a human being almost pales into insignificance. You become de-sensitised to emotions and the personal journey that a candidate goes on. You frankly, couldn't give a shit if their dog died or they have no money to get to an interview, as long as they take the fucking job and secure you your fee.

Do you really want to be *that* kind of recruitment consultant?

I believe the key *has* to be about making it personal. You are not a manufacturing company; you have a pipeline and not a production line. Even if you are flogging tins of beans, you still have to know everything about them in order to sell them. That includes knowing who doesn't like beans, who isn't attracted to the packaging, who hates the sauce and who has gastric problems as well as knowing those who love beans and could frankly eat them cold, straight from the tin.

Yet still recruitment consultant's focus mainly on the things *they* want to focus on when it comes to their candidates:

- Availability
- Skills
- Experience
- Salary/pay rate
- Qualifications
- Travel time
- Achievements

These all translate to "how much money can I make from this candidate?"

And absolutely, you are working to make money, so I don't criticise you for these questions. What I do say is that there needs to be more depth to your questions – much more depth.

If a candidate is lucky then you may ask them about what's important to them in their next role too. Just a thought, but how often do you ask them what they don't want?

Do you ask them what their life situation is like? What they value in life and what part their job plays in that for them?

I'm going to come back to this shortly as there's much more to this.

First things first, are you actually meeting your candidates?

Time and time again I hear from recruitment consultants who don't. Usually reasons are either to do with geography or with urgency. You either physically can't get to see them, or there simply isn't time given the urgency of a role you are working on. Legal documents are scanned and filed and a telephone conversation takes place.

These are more bullshit recruiter excuses and very poor business practice.

It is production line recruitment at its very best in my opinion. With the technology available to us in today's world, there is simply no excuse not to have a face-to-face conversation. Be that one that is *actually* face-to-face or one that takes place using Skype or Facetime. I see no excuse whatsoever to not do this. It goes completely against the grain for me to have a recruitment consultant not meet their candidates (actually or virtually).

If you worked as a sales person for that bean company, do you think that employer would suggest you never actually taste the beans, but just go out and flog them? Surely it would feel weird for you. How can you truly sell the 'bean experience' when you haven't actually tasted the beans?

Besides, how does that behaviour align with your Career Purpose? Do you have one yet? Don't worry if not, we'll take another look at it later. Permit me to assume it *isn't* "To be remembered as a complete snake in the grass, with a cold heart". So with that in mind, how can you ensure you reach that win:win of treating a candidate with the care and concern you should want to treat them with, whilst still ensuring you have what you need to place them?

A face-to-face conversation is a good start. If you've initially had a telephone conversation to ensure you can help then surely that person is then worth seeing face to face? Not only is that more professional but also you both gain so much more from face-to-face interactions. Body language and eye contact are simple, yet essential communication tools that will help you get a true sense of your candidate (and them of you!). That's why I think it's a bullshit response when recruiters suggest they can't meet with candidates because of distance or high volume. It's no wonder there is so little loyalty shown from so many of them. You are simply being shown the same professional courtesy as you've shown them – zero!

So let's assume you've arranged a face-to-face conversation. What are you calling it? A meeting, a chat, a reg, an interview? They all have a place in the world but undoubtedly conjure up different scenarios in the minds of candidates. If you want formality and depth of questioning, call it an interview – oh and you can legitimately tell your clients you have conducted first stage interviews too, bonus! If you want less formal, then a chat or 'reg' (candidates think 'reg' is some random uninvited guy turning up by the way, rather than being short for registration) will do. Be aware you will likely get less effort made in appearance and in answering your questions. I understand that some blue-collar recruiters may be thinking the term 'interview' is too formal for casual workers, so take or leave this advice. At least take heed of my point and the fact you will need to reframe this when you meet to ensure you get what you need.

Alongside the regular questions mentioned earlier on Availability, Skills etc., dig deeper on the candidates driving forces. Find out the things that get them up in the morning, the wider purpose their job/career serves, the personal Values they hold dear. I truly believe that, when we take the time to get under the skin of candidates, we can ensure we really secure them with the opportunities that will serve them for the long term or at very least, offer them fulfilment in their short-term roles.

Treat a candidate interview as you would treat any internal candidate interview rather than asking only things that benefit you, the recruiter. When you focus on really understanding what role is right to meet the needs of your candidate, the money (and your commission) will surely follow. If you follow the money, you'll lose sight of finding great roles for candidates as well as who the candidate is as a person. Doing this will lose you their loyalty and reliability in the long term. Expect to be let down, hear they have changed their mind about work and suddenly be working via other means – and remind yourself you made this happen.

Typically, when I engage with recruiters, they tell me how they have an informal chat when they meet (those that do meet their candidates) and that they can tell within just a few minutes if the candidate will be suitable for their roles. Now either that is super-shrewd recruitment at its finest or there is something else at play here. Given I suspect the latter in the majority of occasions, allow me to elaborate on what the 'something else at play' actually is. It's a sneaky little something called 'unconscious bias'. Have you heard of it? No. Then I'll explain.

Unconscious bias is something each and every one of us has and I refer to it as sneaky because it creeps up on us, often without us realising.

Basically, we make snap judgements on people all of the time. These judgements are based upon our own background, culture and personal experiences. In other words, we tend to 'put people in boxes' based on the aforementioned criteria, making assumptions as we recruit. Whereas I appreciate that all recruiting is in part, based upon subjective opinion, unconscious bias can leave us becoming inadvertently discriminatory. As an example, if a female was looking to register to become a labourer on a building site, what would you do? If you felt this may not be a great culture fit given said building site is male dominated then this is an example of unconscious bias. Based upon your own cultural experience you have made a decision about this individual based upon gender rather than attitude, skills, qualifications and experience. Oh and you've broken the law too! You may have made your judgement with good intention, but broken the law and discriminated against her gender nonetheless.

Just to add insult to injury, there's another sneaky little sonofabitch called 'confirmation bias'. Explained simply, this is the way the human brain likes to be correct. It searches for information to confirm and strengthen our own pre-existing beliefs (sometimes created via *unconscious bias)*. Imagine that same female candidate happened to mention that she 'going out with 'the girls' on a Friday night" even as a throw-away light-hearted remark. If you then find yourself saying silently, "you see, I knew she wouldn't fit that culture, it'll be lipstick and mascara all the way with her" (or words to that effect), then you are exhibiting confirmation bias and reinforcing your own belief that a female would be unsuitable for work on a building site. Get it? If you're still confused then let me ask you how you'd respond if a male candidate had made the equivalent comment about going out with the lads?

I like to think that recruiters do not discriminate, intentionally or otherwise. While this book isn't about the legalities of recruiting (since they change so frequently), you need to be very aware of both unconscious bias and confirmation bias. At best they can blinker you into missing out on great candidates, at worst they can land you up in court on a discrimination charge.

The best way to avoid this is to think, in advance, about the types of questions you will ask your candidates when you meet them. You want to be able to assess and evidence the skills and experience they have in order to know if you have a match. You want to do this fairly and push back against any of your own potential biases in the process. Read on and I'll talk through how best to do this.

If you have researched your market, you should have a general idea of the level of detail your clients will go into when they interview, as well as the types of questions they would ask of the candidates. Test the water about how they'll respond, but similarly give them the opportunity to really demonstrate who they are and what they would bring to a role.

As you'd expect, open questions work well here too. But

more structure provides much more explicit responses. Responses you can really use to market them out to your client base and sell them in to opportunities.

Alongside the *standard* what, who, when, where, why, how questions, consider the typical skills or competencies typically required in the candidate's market, then expand your question portfolio to create CBI (competency-based interview) questions. You may have heard of them. They tend to follow a structure known as the STAR structure, meaning Situation, Task, Action, Result and it goes like this. Imagine the competency you want to assess is problem solving. The question would be structured like so:

Situation: Tell me about a time when

Task: You had to solve a problem

Action: What did you do?

Result: And what was the result?

The reason CBI or STAR questions are so useful is it gets the candidate to really draw from their experience and give you evidence of what they have dealt with. These types of questions avoid having to ask so many hypothetical questions (i.e. what would you do if...), which only give you the subjective thoughts of what a candidate *thinks* they would do. Or rather provide the answer they think you want to hear.

If you asked me what I would do if I found myself dealing with solving a problem, I would know you'd expect me to say I'd keep a cool head, consider the evidence and analyse various possibilities. I'd consult with others and then proceed with a plan to resolve the problem. Therefore I'd probably make up some textbook crap to that effect. Whereas the reality might be that I freaked out, lost my cool completely, shouted a few people down before proceeding with no clear plan and fucking it all up a whole lot more.

The other reason I like them is that, as long as you have decided upon what competencies you want to test, you can use them for every level of candidate. A graduate or school leaver is equally likely to have dealt with problem solving as an individual who has been working professionally for many years.

All that said, many organisations use CBI questions now, so there will undoubtedly be candidates that have mentally lined up some pitch perfect answers. So still they may not always give you a true reflection of who they are.

We find ourselves grappling for more questions to ask. Perhaps it's in order to look good, to kill time and to seem professional. We start to fall into the abyss of dire interview questions, starting with 'what are your strengths and weaknesses?' (Groan), sinking all the way to the bottom of the barrel with 'if you were an animal, what animal would you be and why?' (Vomit). Now I know there are people that will try and justify this excuse for effort as seeing how well people can think on their feet. I say, don't

ask these questions – you sound like a moron. Whenever you ask people about their weaknesses, expect them to answer with things like, "I'm *too* enthusiastic" or "I just *can't* stop work until the job is done". Vague attempts at trying to make strengths sound like weaknesses. I used to say my weakness was chocolate. After all, there are only so many times a person can go along with this shit.

A more effective way to test people is to ask CEQs (Contrary Evidence Questions). As the title suggests, these are questions designed to extract the *contrary* or opposite responses from the previous CBI question.

Still assuming the STAR structure, if we considered problem solving as our competency once more a CEQ would sound like this:

Situation: Tell me about a time when
Task: You were unable to (re) solve a problem
Action: What did you do?
Result: And what was the result?

Notice what a CEQ gives you. Firstly it's also evidence-based (hence the E of CEQ), so the candidate should draw on his/her experiences. Secondly, the answer you receive will give you an insight in to how the candidate reacts when everything isn't going swimmingly. After all, we all have problems and we all have weaknesses. What we as interviewers need to establish, is how well the candidate deals with his/her own when they have to. CEQs will help you push back against those pesky biases too; ensuring your interview process is a fair and balanced one.

A lesser-known type of structured interview question allows us to get even deeper under the surface of your candidate and his/her driving forces, linking to their Values. Needless to say, these are known as VBI (Value Based Interview) questions. The easy part is that they can still follow the STAR structure, but this time you replace the competency with a Value, unsurprisingly. Let's imagine the Value you were looking to assess was *compassion*. The question would be structured something like this:

Situation: Tell me about a time when
Task: You were perceptive of another person's feelings
Action: What did you do (or say)?
Result: And what was the result?

You see how simple interviewing can be when just with a little preparation? How effective it can be? How much easier it will make your role in the long run?
Most importantly, do you see just how much more beneficial these questions are to both you and your clients than the crap that floats around about 'what type of animal you'd be'?

You're welcome.

As you continue through the book you'll see I've added a chapter to support you with an outline structure for a candidate registration interview too, so you can create some order and uniformity for your candidate meetings.

Handy Hint

One of the things you need to do is shift your mind-set from everything going right and change it to one of everything going wrong.

Assuming you have done the *right* things for the *right* reasons, you'll certainly be on the right track with your candidates. But you still also need to protect yourself as much as possible against dropout situations, accepting counter-offers and the like.

I know it's a tough pill to swallow but let's face reality here. We get the sniff of a role; spend a few minutes selling it to the candidate and getting a 'yes', hanging up the phone, high-fiving and mentally spending the commission that will follow. The last thing you want to do is even contemplate anything going wrong. Why would you, you did a mean old sales job didn't you?

And then it happens; you get a call that morning from them (if you're lucky) or a text, moments before they are due to start work. Even worse, the client advises you. It's over – the candidate didn't show, they changed their mind about a role, they accepted a counter-offer. You make a feeble attempt to salvage the situation but it's way too late – it's over. You swear, sulk, rant about what bastards candidates are as you sheepishly remove the fee from the whiteboard, putting the whole experience down to the fact that the candidate was a waste of space.

You remain oblivious to the real reasons behind the situation you find yourself in. In fact, I'd put money on the fact that, even as you read this you'll suggest you did everything I'm about to talk about. I'll suggest you didn't. Why? Because if you had, you'd have noticed warning signs much earlier in the process.

Firstly, did you meet them? No? Well that won't have helped (hence my earlier messages)

Secondly, did you really get under the skin of their driving forces? Really understand what motivates them? Ask a combination of CBI, CEQ and VBI questions when you met them? No? Well then that's another problem.

Now we'll look at my favourite (and most important) 'C' word in recruitment...

Control

Control is *everything* in contingency recruitment and it consistently makes the difference between an average and a great recruiter. If you want to have fewer let downs, fewer counter offers and more placements, then this section is a huge part of what will make the difference for you.

When I said earlier, focus on what could go wrong I meant it. Not to promote a pessimistic mind-set, but instead to ensure you are absolutely, completely, 100% in control of the recruitment process.

Be bold with your candidates and be prepared to hear answers you don't want to hear. Be observant of your candidates. If something doesn't seem right it probably isn't. Be fearless and challenge doubts and hesitations full on. And be brave enough to part company if you remain unconvinced.

All sounds a bit aggressive doesn't it? Internally it should be – do you want your time wasted? No. Do you want to look like an incompetent fool to your client? No. Do you want to work your ass off for something that doesn't convert to a sale? Hell no!

Externally, your aggression is unwanted. Rapport between you and your candidate is still important. Instead, prepare your questions in advance and be assertive, yet professional in your delivery. Here are a few control question examples you should ask:

Who will you discuss your job opportunities with?
What will they advise you?
What will your existing company need to do to keep you?
What will you say when you are counter-offered?
What will make you stay?
What could stop this?
How would you rate this role we're discussing out of 10?
(If not a 10) What's missing for you?

How does this role compare with others you've looked at/been spoken to about/been offered?

Be sure to ask these questions *exactly* as they appear here? Asking 'is there anything that will stop you?' (Probably how you've been asking it), will guarantee a 'no' response. And you'll accept that as a given.

You'll be cursing the bastards when they let you down at the last minute, yet you simply asked the wrong question because you were focusing your attention on what could go right, rather than what could go wrong!

If you're gut suggests all is not right, trust it. It's usually a good judge of character.

Assuming you are still happy that your candidate is a worthy one who can be relied upon, now help both of you by setting some expectations and timelines.

Tell them exactly what will happen next. If you don't have a role for them, then work out a marketing strategy. What companies would they like to work for? What Values and company cultures are important to them? Where do friends and former colleagues work that sounds like somewhere they'd also like to work?

Importantly, for long term contract workers or permanent candidates, also ask them to create a list of things they would bring to a role – reasons an employer should hire them. The more specific the better. The world has quite enough CVs with the generic profiles such as, "I am a great team player who can also work on my own initiative" and the like.

Their job is to be able to define their own positive traits, your job is to be proactive in your marketplace, selling the client the dream, the problem the candidate's skills solve and the added value that the candidate would bring to them as an organisation.

Handy Hint

And yes you are in
service of your
candidates, just as much
as your clients. You may
not invoice your
candidates for your
service, but just try
being a successful
recruiter without them!

Then do what you say you will. It sounds simple, but I'm
still astounded by how often recruiters spout this 'under
promise, over deliver' stuff, yet don't act on it. We can all

talk about it, but if you really care about your work (and the candidates you serve) then you'll take action.

If you do have a role for them? Go through the control questions and propose a timeline for the various parts of the process. Talk them through potential interview stages and dates if you can. Cross check their availability, confirm the need for them to call after interviews with feedback and further questions and be clear about the skills and qualities the client will look for them to demonstrate. You should know by now that a CV only tells a very small part of a candidate's story and it's up to you to coach them through the ways to make each candidate stand out to your client.

If you don't have enough of the above information from the client in order to support your candidates, find out! No you are not a careers advisor, but you are a consultant and consulting means you advise and support your candidates in the art of presenting themselves in the best possible light. Remember, changing jobs is one of the most emotionally draining things we do in life, so 'hold their hand' a little throughout the process. Again it'll reduce the prospect of a last minute let down or 'out of the blue' change of heart.

If the candidate is currently working in a role, take time to talk them through the process of giving notice and handling counter offers. And do that early on and throughout the recruitment process,

not just once. Things change in a candidate's world that recruiters are sometimes unaware of. You need to stay on top of them (metaphorically) every step of the way.

If they aren't currently in work, don't be complacent and assume they will take your job simply because it's a job – they won't. It's still your job to ensure they are 100% happy to start or attend an interview.

Whilst I do accept that a separate book could be written containing all the lame excuses candidates give for not showing up or pulling out of a recruitment process, in the vast majority of cases stones have been left unturned by the recruiter and gut feelings have been ignored.

I speak from a place of experience too – I never always got it right. Hell, I had an 'excuse' given to me once by a temporary candidate that her mother had passed away overnight, the night before a contract was due to start.

Naturally, I was genuinely shocked and saddened to hear such tragic news. I sent flowers, a card and my deepest sympathies to the candidate in question with the promise I'd keep in touch for when she felt ready to consider thoughts of work again. A number of weeks later I called her home to check in on her and was astounded to be told by HER MOTHER that she was out at work!

Years later the sheer audacity of that candidate sticks in my throat, yet if I'm honest, with hindsight, all the signs were there. Inflexibility on start dates, struggles to always get in touch and broken promises when it came to calling me were all there – I had just chosen not to listen to my gut.

That horrid situation – and frankly vile candidate – taught me a valuable lesson. Yes I cursed the candidate. I mean c'mon that has to be one of the most evil excuses ever, right? But from that moment on, I questioned my candidates differently and if there was anything other than certainty in my mind I dealt with it head on. I talked to the candidate about my doubts and showed them I was approachable enough to tell me if they weren't really 'feeling' it. Sometimes, we talked about things and I turned it around, other times not and they were removed from the process until something more suitable came along. But it did stop me looking like a twat in front of my clients and actually strengthened my relationships with both them and my candidates.

As recruiters, we need to take a step back from our own world sometimes and step into the world of others. Different perspectives bring about different outcomes. You work in a people business and so the more you look to understand the way people think the better.

As we conclude this chapter, give some thought to your candidate registration process. What format are you using – telephone, Skype, face to face? What questions are you asking – are you digging 'deep' enough? (Oh and as I've already mentioned, I won't get into the legal stuff around discrimination and protected characteristics, but you should. Record the questions you ask and the answers you receive, (just in case a claim is ever made). What 'control' questions are you asking – could you be asking more?

As I've said, there are no cast iron guarantees when you're dealing with candidates, but following these simple steps will give you the best chance.

To conclude this chapter you may want to consider setting another SMARTASS goal to support your future actions and processes when engaging with your candidates. I'm a helpful (if sometimes curt) soul so here's some space to note it. You're welcome

My SMARTASS goal

_____

_____

_____

_____

_____

Now consider the Step Plan that will follow to ensure your goal is achieved. What is the very next thing that needs to happen to bring your goal to fruition?

My Step Plan (stage one)

_____

_____

_____

_____

_____

What might be some relevant *competencies* to assess through your candidate interview questions?

_____

_____

_____

_____

_____

What might be some relevant *Values* to assess through your candidate interview questions?

Why Clients can be such a nightmare

"Everybody is a Genius. But If You Judge a Fish by Its Ability to Climb a Tree, It Will Live Its Whole Life Believing that It is Stupid"

Albert Einstein

You either already know or are realising quickly, that recruitment is effectively 2 sides of the same coin. Candidates are on one side, with clients on the other.

And boy, can that be a tough coin to toss (although there are some right tossers out there in the market!).

So to be a successful recruiter you have to be able to get the balance right and manage both sides of the coin effectively.

I've been there; we get a sniff of a job, take some basic details and start running around like the proverbial blue-arsed fly to make some calls and send some candidate CVs over. Then getting hugely disappointed (and personally offended) when the match is not right, the brief ends up considerably different to that which we first took, the client pulls the role, or another agency's candidate gets the role. It's frustrating and wastes time. More importantly, you often lose credibility with your client, your candidate (and your boss!).

Once again, you probably find yourself saying, 'I did everything I could', 'that came out of the blue' and other more profane statements. But the real reason it all went wrong; you guessed it – you weren't in control of the process. You looked for everything that would go right, rather than everything that would go wrong.

So what are the best ways to get in control of your clients and your recruitment process? As always, question, question, question. But be sure they are intelligent questions that ensure you get the answers you need.

When the job comes in, take a step back for a moment, slow down and stop getting so excited. I remember seeing a very useful table on LinkedIn a while back, which highlighted the ways to enhance the probability of success.

Questions included:

How long has the job been open for?		
Hot off the press	1-2 weeks	3 weeks+
How many agencies are working on it?		
Exclusive	01-Mar	Everyone working on it!
How many internal candidates are you interviewing?		
None	1	More than 1
How quickly do you need someone?		
Now	1 month	No rush

Notice the more 'ticks' you have in the first column the greater probability you'll fill the job and therefore, the more you should prioritise this role. The more in the last column, the less chance you'll have.

This isn't an exhaustive list by the way, but it's a useful start point in terms of prioritising workload. Consider the key factors that play a role for you and your success. Engage with other colleagues about what would have been useful questions to establish answers to at the start of the recruitment process; and add those to your checklist.

Similarly ask yourself, how often do you meet your clients? If you are working a job for them then you absolutely should have met them, seen their working environment, location etc. If you haven't then you should make it a priority to go and see them. This represents a core part of your recruitment process (or it should), not an after-thought or an 'if I have time' action.

Remember you can get so much from a face-to-face interaction, heightened commitment and honesty for starters. And likewise, your client can get so much from meeting you. If you know, as you should, the Vision and Values of your clients, a meeting also gives you a great opportunity to demonstrate them in the way you operate and to see if they truly live and breathe them as their website suggests.

Those on the client side of the coin have posted many of the recruiter-bashing posts I've seen. Agencies don't listen to what I need, they don't care about my business, they don't call back when they say they will, etc. I'm sure I don't need to remind you the damage it would do to your reputation and that of your employer's, if you were to become the star of one of those online threads.

You want to get into a position where you don't have to justify your fees. But that won't happen overnight.

Handy Hint

It takes initial investment of your time in order to secure the investment of your clients' funds. There is a quote that suggests, 'price is only an issue in the absence of value'. Your job therefore, is to demonstrate value in your service.

Not meeting a client you are working with is another one of those things I consider to be unacceptable. It's shoddy, poor recruitment practice and I simply don't excuse it unless in extreme circumstances.

"What about the clients who I want to meet but who don't have time to meet me?" I hear you ask. The same rule applies. Tell them at the outset that meeting with you, the client who you will be submitting your precious candidates to, is an integral part of your recruitment process. No meeting, no collaboration. Now that may sound harsh, but trust me on this. Recruiting is the responsibility of both you *and* your client. If you are already working in recruitment then do some analysis on the jobs you have filled and had successful relationships with. I'd suggest you have had more success in the long term with those you have met. Besides, how can you possibly sell the role and the company to the candidate if you haven't even been to see the place of work yourself?

And if the client won't budge, then what does that say about his/her commitment to the process? The value they place on staffing? The importance of working in partnership with a recruiter? Not much to be honest. Give yourself and your client the best chance of getting it right first time.

How many times have you been clothes shopping in a rush? There are changing rooms available but you just can't make the extra 5 minutes it'd take to go in, whip your kit off and try the stuff on. You head straight to the checkout, pay and take it home. Only to be devastated to find it doesn't fit. If only you'd taken the time in the first place you'd have actually saved yourself time. Instead you now have to make a second trip to said shop to take it back or change it – all for the sake of that initial 5 minute time investment. It's the same for a client meeting, the initial investment of time from both parties, in order to get the right fit first time.

If you cut corners, you cut commission, end of.

Let's go back to the details you take from your clients about their job. I fully appreciate that in some disciplines, a metaphorical bum on a seat will do. But does that mean you don't need to ask some questions? No, it doesn't.

At very least you need the basics. Core duties and responsibilities, length of assignment (if temp), salary or pay rate, reason for vacancy, hours of work, qualifications etc.

Recruiters tend to then ask about 'person spec' and 'culture fit' but what does that actually mean? The answers you get to these questions should be connected to the Values of the organisation – another important reason to know this at the outset. Challenge what you hear. You may be given generic responses such as 'a team player'. So what's important about teamwork in this role? How will the successful candidate be expected to demonstrate teamwork? How does teamwork reflect the organisational Values? The answers you get now are what are really important. Notice that, as much as is possible, you want to be able to work on objective evidence here, rather than subjective opinion. What one person considers is a great trait for a team player will not necessarily be the same for everyone. Notice how the candidate questions in the previous chapter will help you here too. Yes, in some respects all recruitment is based upon an element of subjectivity, but if you want to make your life easier, ask as many questions as possible that allow you to stick to fact. It's not about being pedantic; it's about having your clients' best interest at heart and doing your utmost to fill the role quickly and with the best person.

Ask questions that delve deeper as to the important competencies required for the role, as well as what Values candidates would be expected to demonstrate.

Alongside the earlier *basic* questions you should additionally be asking further control questions of your clients (especially for permanent roles), unless you want to be taken by surprise by a sudden change. Questions such as:

- What could stop this process?
- How does your interview process work?
- Who is involved in the recruitment/hiring/interview process?
- What is their availability?
- What makes the difference between a good candidate and a great candidate?
- Who is the ultimate decision maker? (Who has the final sign off)
- What *would they* answer to the good candidate/great candidate question?

If you've already sent CVs on spec:

- How would you rate the CV(s) against others you've received? Why?
- What's missing from the CV that you'd need the candidate(s) to demonstrate at interview?

The thing that 99% of recruiters ask when they take a permanent role is 'when do you need them to start?' And typically the client responds with 'ASAP'. In order to truly control the process you should be asking them this question instead; 'When is the latest date you can have someone start in the role?'

Handy Hint

This allows you to create a recruitment schedule with your client. It's a win: win situation as it puts you in complete control yet the client also feels in complete control.

If you also ask the follow up question of "what impact will it have on you/your team/your business if you don't hit that deadline?' you help to create a deeper sense of urgency and commitment.

So what exactly do I mean by a recruitment schedule and how does it help you gain more control?

Well firstly, rather than work from present day forward, it allows you to work from (latest) start date backwards. If you've gained knowledge of the interview process from the client - the stages and structure – you can factor these in. From here you can also factor in feedback dates and times, CV sourcing/advertising time and even potential candidate notice periods to ensure the clients timeline is realistic. If it is, you can then diarise specific dates whereby the particular stage *has* to have happened if the deadline is to be met.

An example could look as follows on the next page:

THE SMARTASS RECRUITER

Job On	CV sent	1st Int	Feedback	2nd Int	Feedback	Offer Accepd	Start Date
1st Aug.	8th Aug.	12th Aug.	15th Aug.	22nd Aug.	25th Aug.	31st Aug.	1st Oct.

There are many things I love about having a recruitment schedule:

1. It creates a realistic achievable timeframe you and the client both agree on
2. You can ensure the client has checked diary and scheduled time out for activities
3. You can pass this schedule on to any candidates in the mix so they know the timeframes to expect
4. It allows the recruiter to forecast financial pipeline more accurately
5. The client is going to be more committed to the process (you have control!)

Et voila, you are in control and the client is also in control.

Naturally if you are running a temp desk then you may not have so many stages in your recruitment schedule. Great! Shortcutting the recruitment cycle is never a bad thing. As long as you're not shortcutting the quality of your service or the commitment of your clients to the recruitment process. Create a system that works for you and your clients and you will undoubtedly strengthen your relationship with them. Consequentially you'll reduce the amount of cancelled projects and changed minds. That *has* to be a useful investment of your time.

Your candidates are also likely to appreciate the heads up on timescales and the expectations you have of them. Chances are few recruiters have ever demonstrated this level of clarity for them so early on in the recruitment process.

Oh and if you do have times when things change beyond anyone's control, then be honest to both sides. The thing people hate more than dealing with a recruiter is dealing with a recruiter who feeds them bullshit. You may think you're the exception who will never be found out. You're not. Those that spout bullshit are always found out, and then...

You guessed it; you just became the star of the latest recruiter rant!

I know it's often all too easy to get bogged down with a hefty workload and that these ideal world strategies can simply go out of the window in the real world. We'll look at this in more detail later on in the book. For now, if you run through in your mind what is driving you to succeed? Your targets, your pay cheque, your Career Purpose, it just might help remind you that a job worth doing is worth doing well.

And on that note, feel free to stick another SMARTASS goal here:

_____

_____

_____

_____

_____

Not forgetting your Step Plan (stage one)

_____

_____

_____

_____

_____

The whites of their eyes

"I wish people would call instead of text and meet instead of call and look into each others eyes instead of each others walls."

Unknown

I've mentioned on several occasions throughout this book just how important it is to meet your clients and candidates.

You know as well as I do that there is nothing that cements a relationship more than actually looking that person in the eye. I have found that, when I speak to many recruiters (especially new recruiters), there is more that holds them back when it comes to face-to-face meetings.

I unfairly thought initially that it was always down to laziness. A corner-cutting exercise born out of the 'I cant be arsed' mentality recruiters are renowned for. And in part that was true (you know who you are!). But for the most part it was way off. Instead I have latterly uncovered, after some deep questioning, that much more frequently the reasons are down to one of two things:

1. A lack of knowledge of how to conduct a meeting, or
2. A lack of confidence in conducting a meeting.

Sometimes there's also a crossover between the two. Knowledge is power right? And in this case, confidence is power too. Let's be clear, if you rock up to a meeting super confident and then quickly demonstrate you don't know your stuff, you are simply not going to get the outcome you'd like.

So let's take a look at how to structure a meeting with a client first. Then we'll go through the principles of the candidate meeting (the registration interview). Finally, I'll provide you with some simple tips on developing confidence – I'm good like that.

I'm choosing to outline the structure of a more formal meeting here. I don't necessarily mean a boardroom-style pitch to several people, but I do mean meetings that are more formalised than the 'pop ins' 'drop ins' that occur. A pop in or drop in will be exactly that. You may be lucky enough to grab 20 minutes of time with a decision maker and that, in some cases, may be all you need. Checking in on a new starter, dropping off branded 'goodies', a coffee and chat all have their place in the recruitment business. Keeping close with your clients and reminding them of your existence and unwavering commitment to them and your candidates on site. But that's not usually how the process starts and the relationship is built. Here I'm talking about getting that initial meeting with a prospective new client. I'm referring to the ways in which you ensure you have every 't' crossed and 'i' dotted, so that you can supply them with what they need whilst successfully convincing them of your competence to do so.

We'll assume that you have asked for the meeting on your call, received agreement; we'll go from there.

My advice would firstly be to send an email confirming the date and time of the meeting, highlighting who will be

 present from your company and from theirs, together with the expected duration of the meeting. An agenda of what will be discussed. The memory still haunts me of the occasion I bobbed off to meet a client, expecting just to see him. I walked in to the meeting room to see 5 other managers sat down and waiting to be 'wowed' by me! I was neither mentally nor physically prepared. I'd brought with me one of everything, one business card, one brochure and one company mug. I felt like a twat and although I partly salvaged my blushes throughout that meeting, it was certainly an experience I didn't wish to repeat. Sending an agenda in advance would definitely have helped in confirming the attendees in advance. Now I swear by them.

Another benefit of an agenda is, through choosing to note the time *and* duration of the meeting on it, you are less likely to prepare for an hour and find out latterly your client only has half that amount of time!

The other obvious thing an agenda provides is a structure for the meeting. The information that will be covered by you, as well as that which will be required from your client. Simple pre-preparation which will have you and your client feeling more relaxed about the proceedings. It also allows for them to add something else to the agenda *before* the meeting takes place. Again, it allows you time to prepare and avoid potentially embarrassing surprises.

Sending an agenda, an agenda the client has had the opportunity to review, will mean you have fewer cancelled or postponed meetings. Given it's hard enough to manage time, this is an unexpected bonus for a recruiter.

But the best thing an agenda provides you with is a prompt. Once confirmed, print off a copy for you and all attendees to distribute on arrival and voila, you have a visual prompt sheet to remind you what to say. No more, "I wish I'd asked this" or "I forgot to check on that" situations. No more bollockings from your manager about the very same, when you arrive back into the office. No more having to sheepishly call your client back to 're-confirm' information you really should have obtained. Agendas are awesome!

And the structure? Well that's the easy part. Remember your role in sales in to solve problems. In order to do that you need to obtain information through intelligent questions. This concept itself should give you a clue as to the base structure to follow:

- Introductions
- About them (company, recruitment, challenges)
- About you (company, solutions you can offer)
- Handle any blockers and negotiate as may be necessary
- Close with some form of commitment

You see – it's just like telephone selling. No drama. Naturally there will be much more to each agenda as is pertinent to your recruitment sector and you client's business, but you get the general idea.

What *is* important to consider with face to face meetings is there is nowhere to hide. In other words, you should feel confident enough that you know your marketplace well, have considered the solutions you can offer to any issues and also confirmed with your  boss what authority you have to negotiate. Although it's not completely the end of the world to have to 'come back to them' on something, you don't want to spoil your good work by looking like a twat. Neither do you want to make it up as you go along. Bullshit won't get you far (and you know how much I despise bullshit in business).

Notice how having an agenda, a structure and some things prepared in advance of your meeting already gives you some added confidence. Now let's think about how you can boost that further.

Prepare, prepare, prepare.

Part of the fun of a recruiters' life is the busy nature of the work. Lots going on, balls to juggle, plates to spin. A level of variety that makes the role both fabulous and frustrating in equal measure. But what that often leads to when it comes to meetings, is rushing around and dashing out of the door at the last minute. Secretly many of you love that, the stockbroker style of 'buy buy sell sell', grabbing a merchandise pack whilst balancing a sandwich between your teeth and racing to the car park with moments to spare. But you are not a stockbroker, you are a consultant, a so-called expert in your field (no offence stockbrokers) and experts take time to get themselves physically and mentally prepared for proceedings.

A meeting with your client will be one of a series of those 'touches' I referred to earlier on. You will likely have made *at least* one telephone call to them prior to meeting. You will have some information about them and their business. Please, please check this before you leave the office. I had an occasion once whereby I was being a 'stockbroker' recruiter, dashing out of the office door having left everything much too late. I simply forgot to check my system notes beforehand and thought I could just wing it (as we do). One of my opening questions to my client was something I consider mortifying to this day.

We made small talk on the way from reception to his office and then I dropped my bombshell. "So, tell me about your business" I said. If you can visualise the most pissed off face of a client possible, I assure you it's not as pissed off as his face was that day. He responded with this (it still sends a chill through me), "you ask to come to MY office, ask for MY time to discuss MY business and you don't know what we do?" Now, clearly I *did* know. I had just left all the information on the bloody system back in the office! Needless to say, he terminated the meeting and asked me to leave. It was quite possibly the worst experience of my recruitment life. I'm only glad that LinkedIn didn't exist at that point. I would undoubtedly have become the 'star' of that rant.

And quite rightly too.

 It was inexcusable that I was so unprepared and I completely deserved his wrath. All because I hadn't allowed just those few extra minutes to check in and confirm the details I needed.

When you appoint a meeting, diarise time to prepare for it as well as travel to it. Print off your notes if you can to take with you. It shows the client clearly how well you've prepared. Double-check the route you'll be taking and the time it should take you before you leave. Also confirm the location address and postcode for the site. I've driven to Royal Mail sorting offices on more than one occasion, inadvertently following the post code for a P.O. box! And for God's sake, switch off your phone before you step in. I had yet another embarrassing experience once when I forgot and my ringtone rendition of 'bananas in pyjamas' blasted out of my bag as I was in mid-flow talking with a company Director! Luckily he took it in his stride and laughed, but I'm sure that was more to save my blushes than down to the fact that he actually found it funny.

Consider what you'll take with you when you prepare. A selection of CVs are a must (or candidate profiles if they don't have CVs). CVs represent your product, so why wouldn't you showcase them. If I worked for Cadbury's (a girl can dream) and came to meet you without bringing you a chocolate bar, that would be a bit weird wouldn't it? So why would you ever go to meet one of your clients without a sample of your product? You don't necessarily need to give them all to your client, but have them to hand so you can if it's appropriate.

What else will you take with you? Paper and pens (take two pens in case one runs out), laptop or tablet, business cards, brochures, your terms of business and some testimonials of your work.

Handy Hint

Testimonials or referrals of your work are evidence of your competence (that social proof we looked at earlier) and it's always good to demonstrate this at a meeting.

Have objectives for your meeting. It shouldn't just be a general follow up to your phone calls. You should have a purpose to the meeting, outcomes that you'd like to achieve through the interaction. Otherwise, why bother?

What about meeting candidates?

When you arrange to meet with your candidates (as I hope you will do now), it's equally important to have a structure, a visual prompt even, to ensure you get everything you need and support you placing your candidates.

Be sure you have arranged a suitable place to meet, one where there is adequate space and few distractions. Decide upon the competencies you will want to assess in advance so you feel organised and don't end up going off on lots of multiple tangents. Before you begin your meeting, check how much time your candidate has. It may be they have an hour on the car park. You need to know what time you have at the outset. If you are on Skype, be sure you have a decent wifi connection.

Talk through the structure of the meeting. Many candidates will feel nervous and your job is to put them at ease. If they know what's coming that will help.

Your base structure should be something like this:

- Introductions
- Who you are and what you do (in brief)
- Run through timings and structure of the registration interview
- Talk through CV (generally most recent role first, qualifications, skills), Discuss any incomplete dates and gaps in employment
- Competencies – CBIs, CEQs and VBIs
- Discuss any open roles you have and their suitability
- Ask your control questions!
- Explain your expectations of them
- Explain what they can expect from you and your company (marketing plans, availability, payment methods etc.)
- Agree next steps, thank them and close

Despite the assumption that recruiters are good interviewers, I meet many who really have very little structure to their candidate meetings and therefore rely wholly on subjective opinion, as well as the unconscious and confirmation biases we looked at earlier in the book. Give yourself the best chance of getting everything you need right at the outset.

If you don't think you can help a candidate or don't believe they are suitable for a role, tell them. Candidates loathe recruiters who keep them hanging on and are dishonest by omission. LinkedIn here they come! Provide honest feedback – that's what you'd want

Personal presentation

Now think about yourself. How are you dressing for the meeting? Is it appropriate attire for your audience and (I hope this goes without saying) is it clean and tidy? How are you personally 'groomed'? Be careful not to drown yourself in perfume or aftershave. If the client or candidate doesn't like it, it can be off-putting. If you're a smoker, don't smoke just prior to a meeting. Whether you chew gum or eat toothpaste afterwards, you will still smell of smoke. If you are worried about 'shaky' hands, consider if you will or won't accept a drink if offered. Make sure you've been to the loo beforehand too to save you fidgeting in your seat. Not a great look!

Before your meeting, whether you are driving or travelling on public transport, even on foot; think about your Career Purpose and your Values. Be sure you keep repeating them to yourself so that you keep them at the forefront of your mind. They will help you keep focused on your outcomes and your behaviours throughout.

This meeting is a small part of your journey towards fulfilment.

It matters.

Handy Hint

Take some time to
concentrate on your
breathing. The deeper
you breathe, you'll
notice the more relaxed
you will become. This
will allow you to take
your time and pace your
voice throughout the
meeting.

Consider your posture en-route to and during the meeting. Are you slouching, dragging your feet and slumping your shoulders? Or are you walking 'tall', sitting up straight and maintaining open body language. Notice how, when you do this, you feel more confident and self-assured but without coming over as too cocky. Confident and self-assured is a great way to come across to clients in meetings. Cocky most definitely isn't a good look. You know what confident 'looks' like don't you? Before you leave this chapter just play with that concept for a moment. Stand in a confident pose and hold it for a couple of minutes. Notice how you actually start to feel more confident!

Whether you feel confident first and then change posture, or whether in fact you change your posture first and then feel confident it really doesn't matter. If you remain unconvinced, Google a great TED Talk by Amy Cuddy 'How your body language shapes who you are' and you'll see exactly what I mean (great tips for your candidates for their interviews too!).

In conclusion, be prepared both mentally and physically for a client meeting. Plan your timings, send an agenda, know your market and take the appropriate collateral (and CVs). This helps with the structure.

Have your objectives and Career Purpose at the forefront of your mind, breathe deeply and adopt open 'confident' body language. This will support enhancing your confidence.

Meetings are a crucial and worthwhile activity for recruiters. Enjoy them and get the most from every opportunity. You might just surprise yourself.

Perhaps you'd like to consider your own client and candidate meeting structure?

As you've come to expect, I like to promote action.

So there's some space on the next pages for you to make a start.

Client Meeting

Candidate Registration Interview

Sort my own shit out

"The same boiling
water that softens
the potato, hardens
the egg.
It's about what you'r
madeof, not the
circumstances."

Unknown

THE SMARTASS RECRUITER

If you're a typical recruiter then you simply don't have enough hours in the day.

If it's not emails to respond to, it's candidates to call, market, ensure are legally compliant, meet and arrange interviews for. It's clients to call, prospect, take job details from or go out and meet. It's managers to send reports to, kpi info, pipeline forecasts. Or it's attending internal meetings (about very little mostly).

How does a recruiter fit everything in? I mean we all have the same amount of hours in the day don't we? So why is it that many recruiters seem to struggle so much with time management?

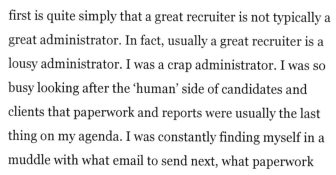

I have a number of theories here. The first is quite simply that a great recruiter is not typically a great administrator. In fact, usually a great recruiter is a lousy administrator. I was a crap administrator. I was so busy looking after the 'human' side of candidates and clients that paperwork and reports were usually the last thing on my agenda. I was constantly finding myself in a muddle with what email to send next, what paperwork went with what and which work to prioritise. Whenever I was asked about what topic I'd like to explore from a personal development perspective, I often responded with *anything* other than time management. It's a boring and dull topic at best and not at all a sexy aspiration for a top class recruiter.

The second theory is that recruitment is both proactive and reactive by nature. How is it even possible to 'time manage' that which cannot be predicted? All the planning in the world couldn't prepare me for the unknown, so why bother in the first place. And 'planning' by nature is another administration task – boring!

The third theory is that no one actually gives a shit about your workload. The manager who calls a meeting to discuss 'figures' even though the very same figures can all be accessed via the CRM. Besides the figures probably haven't changed a whole lot since yesterday's meeting about figures! The candidate who calls for a quick catch up, right in the middle of your core business development time, seemingly about very little (remember Janice?). The colleague who wants to catch up on GOT from last week, as they missed it. None of these people mean to distract or hinder your progress. They just don't give a shit.

THE SMARTASS RECRUITER

My final theory is that recruiters are lazy. Now that, I know, is a profound statement. One that sounds rather negative in its connotations. But in many ways, laziness is a positive trait in recruitment. As long as you're *smart lazy*. Anything else and you need to get your finger out of your ass and work.

The smart lazy recruiter on the other hand, is the one that looks for the simplest, quickest and most effective way to do something. The one who stands up for themselves about whether that aforementioned meeting is necessary. The one who, at the start of the process, makes it clear to their candidates when they are available (and unavailable) to talk. The one who is disciplined enough to hold off on TV and random chat until the key important work is complete. The one who goes all out to short cut the recruitment process through control (see previous chapters) and is less likely to run around like a blue-arsed fly forgetting things as they go. That's smart lazy.

I, and many like me, have seen and delivered many techniques for managing time. To-do lists, Covey's Important/Urgent Matrix*, saying 'no' to others more. Time stealers, time bandits or time monkeys – whatever the buzz phrase is at the time.

Truth is, when it comes to time management, there are no magic wands, no potions, no theories and no methods that are 100% on the money. They all have their place and are useless in equal measure.

Sure, a to-do list is great. It's a simple way to note everything that needs doing (and beats 30 post-it notes randomly scattered over your workspace). Sure, prioritising those tasks using Covey's Important/Urgent Matrix is a useful way to decide which of those tasks to do first. Sure, knowing when you can legitimately say 'no' to something (or someone) is worth considering.

But HELLO, this is real world recruitment. This is a role where things can change direction (often rapidly) on a sixpence and before you know it, all those lists and best

---

* see Stephen Coveys book, The Seven Habits of Highly Effective People

laid plans have frankly gone to shit. You write and re-write your to-do list (taking up more time), you find yourself prioritising your priorities. And that attempt at saying 'no' almost gets you fired.

So what the hell is a recruiter supposed to do to become (more) efficient?

Honestly, the best advice I can give you here is this:

Plan for what you *can* plan for. Those things that are the same; week in week out, month in month out. Diarise them and set reminders. Then remember to check your diary reminders!

Timesheet and payroll deadlines for example; weekly team meetings. Anything that you know will not change each week. Stick time for that in your calendar or add to your to-do list.

Stay close to the money. Taking interview feedback for a potential immediately starting booking is closer to the money than sending an email to a prospective client. Prioritise accordingly.

The rest? Well that's for you to get sensible about. And I don't mean that to sound condescending, instead more realistic. Stop telling candidates to 'call anytime' if you're not going to be available all the time. Instead give them a sensible time 'window' when they can call and have your undivided attention. Then make sure you're there to take the call! Allocate some time each week that typically works for you to be out of the office, meeting clients or candidates. And stick to it as rigidly as you can. Communicate what you're doing with your line manager to ensure they are on board. Diarise follow up calls as they happen so you can always see what calls need making in advance. Tell your colleagues when you need space to focus on work, rather than TV chit chat.

And keep your Career Purpose in mind. If that task doesn't serve you in the long term, maybe you should question doing it. If it does serve you, then find the most effective way to do it and get it off your list. That doesn't mean just not doing stuff that needs doing, but your time is valuable and what you get from each day is basically down to you and you alone.

The questions that follow might be a bit 'out there' and possibly even a bit confusing. But if you're really stuck when something threatens your time, ask yourself them:

- *What will happen if I do this?*
- *What won't happen if I do this?*
- *What will happen if I don't do this?*
- *What won't happen if I don't do this?*

As a recruiter you're expected to be a sales person and an administrator. But first and foremost, you're in service of  others. Being organised doesn't mean you have to become the office bore, but likewise being the joker of your team won't get the job done. Being organised doesn't mean spending precious hours each day planning, but likewise if your workstation is cluttered and you make no use of automated calendar and diary functions, you fail to allow for the things that happen each and every week and then you're setting yourself up for a fall.

And perhaps most importantly remember that fundamentally, no one gives a shit about you. Giving a shit at work is something only you can do. Selfishly and unashamedly. It's a choice we make every morning as the alarm wakes us up as well as every time we step in to the office and every time something (or someone) threatens our time.

There's little point in stressing about time. Stuff will happen anyway. If you have other people in your team who can help and support you (and they are willing to help) then that's great. But ultimately in recruitment your success is down to one person and that person is you.

Those who want it more will succeed at sorting their shit out. Simple.

So in conclusion, you just have to want it more.

I'll let you create your own action plan here, if you have time!

My Action Plan

Daily Tasks	Weekly Tasks	Monthly Tasks

Owning that sale

"The key to successful sales is the ability to ask intelligent questions."

Jackie Handy

What makes one recruiter different from another?

Depends who you ask.

People will always make judgements on us. In many ways (and as the quotes suggest) what others think about us is none of our business. To an extent I agree with this principle. However, when it's your reputation on the line you should be aware of what makes you different and also feel confident that others see that difference in your behaviours and actions.

Whenever I ask recruiters the question, "what makes you different?" I get answers that typically reflect tangible things offered by their employer. Things like;

- We meet all our candidates
- We offer various types of work
- We put our clients first

And so on.

And I say, "meh".

Why? Because those things are quite superficial really. They are also rather generic and when something is generic it isn't what makes you different is it? It's what makes *everyone* different. That means everyone is fundamentally the same.

My question was "what makes *you* different?" I want to know how you work differently to all you colleagues. Why you are unique when compared to all the other thousands of recruiters across the globe. That creates a very different mind-set doesn't it?

Try asking yourself the question this way, "On your best day, what do you love about your job?"

Or how about this, "how do you make a difference to those you serve?"

The processes contingency recruiters follow is roughly the same. The offerings from all recruitment companies are vaguely similar. You are often the only true USP (Unique Selling Point) on offer in your business. So if you can't articulate that, then how do you stand out to your network?

Throughout this book I've talked a lot about Career Purpose and how important it is to have something clear in your mind that helps you shape the work you do and the success of that work.

It took me a long time to realise my Career Purpose. Other stuff got in the way constantly. The next month's pay cheque, hitting my targets, pleasing my boss. Yet so often I got to the end of each month feeling emotionally unfulfilled. I may have had cash in the bank; I may have been top of the league tables. But all this was short lived. You know as well as I do that in sales you are only as good as your last month's figures. The very nature of that concept is emotionally unfulfilling isn't it? All those previously great months mean jack shit if the next month is a poor sales month.

So how do recruiters keep themselves going?

Firstly, you need to truly understand your key strengths. Often these go hand in hand with the things you love about your role. Maybe you just love meeting people. Chances are then that you'll be a recruiter who books in lots of client visits and candidate interview registrations. Perhaps you love working quickly. Then the chances are you'll be constantly busying yourself with candidate and client calls.

Great, you probably find yourself regularly exceeding those KPIs.

Secondly though (and this is really important), you need to recognise your weaker areas. In the training room I tend to call these you *development areas,* as I hate the term 'weakness', but whatever you call them, you need to be aware of them.

We do more of what we love – that's human nature plain and simple. We spend most of our time perfecting this to the best of our ability. Yet on the journey we often avoid giving time to the things we either enjoy less or are less capable of doing.

So you may be that recruiter who gets lots of meetings with clients, but do you really ask them the right questions? Do you secretly enjoy the niceties of conversations but lack a robust structure of intelligent questions to ask them that will help you both in the long term?

Maybe you are the recruiter that candidates love, the one that has endless conversations with them about their lives and really shows an interest in them. But are you really getting under the skin of what they want in work? Are you then able to successfully find them the work that allows them to fulfil their own needs?

Maybe you do love working quickly, but does that mean you're working in a paper swamp, with an untidy desk, wasting endless hours searching through the piles of paperwork and post-it notes in order to get anything done?

The points I'm making are that, whilst you can enjoy something it doesn't automatically mean you're doing it as effectively as you can. Furthermore if your focus is simply on playing a numbers game, that won't automatically make you a great recruiter.

I asked a relatively new recruiter recently that question. "How do you make a difference to those you serve?" He sheepishly told me, "I change people's lives". He then apologised for giving such a feeble and fluffy sounding response. Yet for me that response was one of the most profound I'd heard. That was true Career Purpose. Everything that recruiter did each day was focused around how he was changing people's lives.

And that made all the difference to the quality of both his input and output at work.

When he spoke with his candidates, he dug deeper to truly understand the change they were looking for in their lives and how the right work would create this reality.

When he spoke to clients, he investigated hard on what difference the right employee would make to the business and the life of the employer themselves. He understood what was currently missing for them and how that affected them.

Knowing he was a 'life changer' meant he had to operate in an organised, tidy fashion. He had to act quickly and efficiently.

He had to make expectations and intentions clear to candidates, clients *and* his colleagues in order to fulfil this.

What this clear Career Purpose also allowed for him was to be able to look at his results, analyse his performance and be open-minded enough to constantly evolve to ensure he could change more and more lives month on month.

As an example of this 'evolution', he recognised that whilst he got lots of jobs to work on from clients, he was too reliant on the candidate CV to sell them in. He knew the important things the candidate needed from a role. He'd investigated well around what they could bring to a role. Yet all too often these things weren't immediately apparent on the candidate CV and he wasn't securing many interviews for them.

He was initially so wrapped up in getting CVs over to the client quickly that he omitted some of the key differentiators the candidate possessed. He forgot, in his haste to please the client, to actually highlight to the client the (less tangible) ways in which his candidates could make a difference to the client and the client's business.

He was forgetting to bridge the gap.

Once he'd analysed his ratios. His Job on: Job filled ratio and his CV sent: Interview ratio, he realised his mistake. Moving forward he worked with each candidate to draft a paragraph on 'how they would make a difference' and included that with each CV he sent. Furthermore, he added his own additional passage for the client explaining the reasons they should meet his candidates.

Just a few more minutes of analysis, open-mindedness, the humility to change, followed by intelligent working practises made all the difference. Keeping his, "I change people's lives" Career Purpose clear he saw a significant increase in his results. More interviews, more jobs filled, more lives changed. Including his own life of course.

Consequentially he made more commission and this enabled him to provide for his family in a way he hadn't previously been able to. As a result, he exceeded his KPIs, rose to the top of the league tables consistently (and naturally, pleased his boss).

The moral of this story isn't about results. It's about emotional fulfilment. This recruiter was engaged in his work, took pride in what he did, focused on those he served. His Career Purpose kept him going through the shit days, through the times when things didn't run smoothly or go to plan (which happens frequently in recruitment).

His strategy needed to change in order to ensure his success, but his Career Purpose never wavered.

Handy Hint

That's how you 'own the sale'. Recognise the value in everything you do. When you work in a people-centric business it has to be personal. Treat people like numbers and they will act like numbers, treat them with empathy and genuine care and you'll get much more from your work in recruitment.

Get into the habit of analysing your results through your ratios. Understand what makes a *strong* ratio in your organisation. Some ratios you might want to consider are:

- Calls made to Jobs taken
- Jobs taken to Jobs filled
- CVs sent to Interview (or start)
- Jobs offered to start
- Candidates registered to placed

Don't forget your financial aspirations too (I'm sure you won't!). Consider your average invoice values or average margins. What percentage of your bookings are you discounting (are you dropping your pants)? What difference would it make to your billed revenue and your pay cheque, if you discounted fewer bookings? Could you increase your fees slightly and, if so, how would that help you hit and exceed your targets quicker? What difference would that make to your career? To your life?

Have the strength of character to be able to identify the things you do because you enjoy them, but also the things you do well. You need to repeat these and ensure your strengths remain strengths. But also be humble enough to acknowledge your shortcomings. The things you do less well and the things you avoid doing because you enjoy them less. These are the things that need to change. These are your gaps to bridge.

Don't let arrogance or pride get in your way of emotional

fulfilment. To be a cocky recruiter takes a whole lot fewer balls than to be a recruiter who is committed to his/her own development through consistently analysing and evolving their strategic approach.

Be reminded of the ASS in your SMARTASS goals. If you are to truly to achieve your goals you need to remember the Alignment with your wider Career Purpose. You need to swallow the pill that nothing gets achieved without a level of Sacrifice. It might be time that you have to sacrifice, or it might be your pride. Either way, it's an essential part to achieving your goals. Finally remember, no man (or woman) is an island. You will need some level of Support in order to evolve. From your candidates, from your clients or from your colleagues. Don't ever be afraid (or too proud) to acknowledge that and state what you need. Remember that you too have the power to change lives. Your life and the lives of others.

Repeating the process

"An investment in knowledge always pays the best interest."

Benjamin Franklin

I've worked with hundreds of recruiters. New recruiters as well as those that have worked in the industry for many years. I've also been a recruiter for many years, I've made lots of mistakes and I've done a lot of things right.

The years have taught me that the easy part to recruitment is actually understanding the art of recruitment. Recruitment isn't rocket science. You match a candidate with a job and a job with a candidate right? Simple.

The hard part is consistency. It's being resilient when everything feels like it's going to shit. It's remembering the basic fundamentals of the role years after you began this career. Its evaluating what works and what doesn't. Most importantly it's remembering that this is a people business. People are not tins of beans. They are all different and therefore they all command a different approach. People don't (or shouldn't) have labels attached to them. They all have different 'ingredients'; skills, qualifications, experience and stories that make them unique.

The real skill of a recruiter is to keep complexity simple. I know right, strange statement. Let that sink in for a moment; keep complexity simple.

Accept that people *are* different and frequently contradict norms. All accountants are not equal, nor builders, nor IT professionals, nor recruiters.

This book contains information about tried and tested processes. Techniques that, when followed consistently, will work to support you succeed in  recruitment. If you haven't already you'll likely start putting some of these techniques into practice soon and you'll see for yourself. This book will have paid for itself a hundred times over.

But then you'll forget about the book (just like those training workbooks). You'll find yourself starting to revert back to old habits, cutting corners that should never be cut, cracking under the pressure of sales targets, KPIs and a manager who thinks their way is better. You'll begin to treat people like tins of beans again just because one 'bad egg' let you down. You'll start making simplicity complex, rather than the other way around.

So keep this book close by. Read it again in 12 months and notice what you're doing and not doing. Notice what's changed for you.

Look at the notes you made throughout this book (you made notes didn't you?) and monitor the progress you've made towards your SMARTASS goals.

There are several technical messages throughout this book including:

Planning – your strategy, call lists, goals, your time.
Differentiation – yourself and in your 'why you do what you do'. Differentiation in your marketing, your advertising and your service.
Selling - your technique, intelligent questioning, identifying what's missing for both your clients and your candidates, telephone and face-to-face communication
Control – the control of your time, the recruitment process, your own performance analysis
Concentrating your efforts in all of these areas will certainly support you in accelerating your performance as a recruiter. I worked in operational recruitment for well over a decade. It was years into my career that I really pieced together this jigsaw and I wish I'd done so years before.

But to really and truly give yourself the edge as a recruiter I trust you have taken the additional messages away from this book too:

Service – recruitment is a service industry and you are in service of your candidates and clients. Never forget this.

Personal – you get from this job what you put in. Make your service bespoke, your empathy genuine and your efforts sincere. Take care of yourself so you can take care of your customers.

SMARTASS – you probably gathered this was an important message throughout this book! Consider the goals you set for yourself carefully. Consider what you really want to achieve and the amount you are prepared to give (and sacrifice) in order to achieve them.

Take care of the above and you'll go far. You'll experience financial benefits through increased placements and repeat business. You'll get yourself known through the industry as someone who provides value. Someone who truly humanises the recruitment process. You'll achieve so much more in your work through setting out clear, considered Step Plans designed to support you moving forward day by day, one step at a time.

If all recruiters do this, the shitty reputation currently attached to this great industry begins to gradually shift to a more positive one.

This book isn't designed to provide an overnight fix to everything, but perhaps it's helped you re-evaluate *what* you will do and *how* you will do it. Perhaps it's helped give you some clarity on *why* you do what you do and the steps you'll take to achieve what you want to achieve. When ethical working practices are well executed, we recruiters provide real value to our customers and you have the power (and the tools) to make that happen.

To conclude with a cliché; in recruitment you get out what you put in, you reap what you sow, karma's a bitch. Take your pick, but you get the idea.

The recipe for success isn't just doing *things right*; it's also about doing the *right things*. So go ahead and be a SMARTASS and do it unashamedly.

Before you know it you'll be promoted and venturing into the world of management.

And that my friends, is a whole different ball game...

Extra Notes Pages

Extra Notes Pages

Extra Notes Pages

Extra Notes Pages

Extra Notes Pages

Extra Notes Pages

Extra Notes Pages

Extra Notes Pages

Lightning Source UK Ltd.
Milton Keynes UK
UKHW020627090120
356645UK00011B/804/P